# Sex Education Books for Young Adults 1892–1979

# Sex Education Books for Young Adults 1892–1979

**PATRICIA J. CAMPBELL**

R. R. BOWKER
COMPANY

New York & London, 1979

Published by R. R. Bowker Company
1180 Avenue of the Americas, New York, N.Y. 10036
Copyright © 1979 by Xerox Corporation
All rights reserved
Printed and bound in the United States of America

**Library of Congress Cataloging in Publication Data**

Campbell, Patricia J
  Sex education books for young adults, 1892–1979.

  Bibliography: p.
  Includes index.
    1. Sex instruction—United States—History—
Bibliography. 2. Sex customs—United States—History—
Bibliography. 3. Youth—United States—Sexual
behavior—History—Bibliography. I. Title.
Z7164.S42C35  [HQ35]  016.30141′8′055  79-1535
ISBN 0-8352-1157-6

# CONTENTS

# PREFACE

*The willingness of the adult world to share with young people whatever accurate and valid information on sexual and reproductive behavior we possess constitutes one of our best gestures of confidence and communication in their direction.*—DR. MARY CALDERONE

*Sex Education Books for Young Adults, 1892–1979* is an analysis of sexual advice literature for American teenagers from the late Victorian era to the present. The history of the sex education book documents the almost unconscious movement of our culture's ideas and attitudes toward sex and youth; it reveals both the heritage of our own sexual beliefs and the foundation for contemporary codes of behavior. As this study makes abundantly clear, the one distinguishing feature that has characterized sex education for young people in America from Victorian to modern times has been the reluctance of parents, sex educators, and other professionals to tell teenagers what they really need and want to know about sex. Indeed, from their first appearance, sex education books for young adults have aimed primarily at preventing teenagers from engaging in any sexual activity outside of marriage.

While the theme of sex prevention is most blatant in the earlier manuals, as recently as the 1960s sex education books continued to emphasize the dangers of venereal disease and illegitimate pregnancy rather than the cure and prevention of these conditions. Generation after generation of American teenagers have been taught to fear and deny the impulses of their own bodies. Much of the source for the just but destructive anger that hampers the Women's Movement can be found in the sex instruction manuals of the fifties.

The authors of these books were not conscious villains; they simply reflected the attitudes and apprehension of our fundamentally "sex negative" society. Only in the past few years have sex educators begun to acknowledge teenage sexuality to the point of providing young people with the considerate advice and practical information they need to live safely and responsibly. Today, a sex education book that is older than ten years is a road map to a country that no longer exists. It is precisely because sexual ideas are in a state of constant flux that libraries and other agencies that provide sex education books for young people must continually reevaluate, weed, and add to their collections.

Sex education books for teenagers are a true literary genre—they show "a distinct style, form, and content" as the dictionary specifies. Whether the tone is pompous or jazzy, the intent is always to teach teenagers the currently approved sexual behavior for their age group. The content is a combination of anatomical and medical information and ethical exhortation, with the proportions varying according to fashion and each author's expertise. In the few cases in which a book discusses only ethics or only physiology, the author has usually felt it necessary to justify the one-sidedness of his or her approach. Despite such variations, the genre can be seen as a unique type with its own conventions and even its own jargon (surely the word "petting" was never used in ordinary speech).

The historical development of the sex education book is internally consistent. The authors imitated each other shamelessly, making minor revisions to the established pattern of advice, while offering their own works as the first adequate books on the subject. With enthusiastic scorn they often denounced their predecessors' work as worthless and even vicious. Nevertheless, the current of prevailing social opinion is quite accurately mirrored in these books, and even minute changes in society's position can be detected in the adjustments made in successive editions of a particular title.

*Sex Education Books for Young Adults, 1892–1979* is arranged chronologically, with each chapter covering roughly a decade. The last chapter is an annotated bibliography of books this author considers to be currently valid, and is intended to provide help for librarians, teachers, youth workers, and parents in their task of choosing the best sex education books for teenage needs. This section also provides a list of evaluation tools for keeping that selection up to date.

Although a few textbooks are included as typical examples, and an occasional pamphlet is examined when it is historically significant or representative of a trend, the focus of this study is the true sex education handbook written for the private reading of young people in their teens. Excluded are books addressed to children or college students, books for parents or educators about teenage sex, and books limited to special topics such as venereal disease or rape. The eighty-seven year span represented in the title encompasses the life history of the form. As explained in Chapter 1, although advice manuals for married couples and for single men and women in their twenties had become common as early as the 1830s, the sex education book written expressly for teenagers' reading did not emerge as an independent form until the end of the nineteenth century.

Because neither a comprehensive library collection nor a comprehensive bibliography exists on the history of sex education books for young adults, the research for this volume involved examination of the subject catalogs and holdings of numerous institutions, including the library of the Institute for Sex Research of Indiana University (the Kinsey Institute), the research libraries of the University of California at Los Angeles and the University of Southern California, the Los Angeles City Public Library, and the Los Angeles County Medical Library. Also consulted were *Cumulative Book Index* and the *National Union Catalog*, which was useful in locating those books that were not available in the above libraries but that could be borrowed through the Interlibrary Loan Department of Los Angeles Public Library. A visit to the Library of Congress was the final step in the research process, where a number of titles unobtainable elsewhere were examined.

The evaluation and selection of sex education books will continue to be among the most sensitive decisions that face parents and all professionals who work with young people. As this history amply demonstrates, the withholding of accurate, helpful information about human sexuality represents a serious disservice to youth. The task remains, however, not only to choose the best books available at any given time, but to ensure the accessibility of those works to their intended readers.

# ACKNOWLEDGMENTS

I wish to express thanks to Audrey Eaglen, who published my article in the Winter 1977 issue of *Top of the News* that became the basis for this book, and who offered warm encouragement. I am also indebted to librarians Melvin Rosenberg, who supported my initial research, and Jane Bevier, who believed in me. The rest of the staff of the Los Angeles City Public Library, especially Vivian Mott and Lillian Clary of the Interlibrary Loan Department, were tireless in tracking down rare and obscure volumes. The staff of the library of the Institute for Sex Research of Indiana University were kind and helpful in making their magnificent collection accessible. Finally, I am grateful to Mary K. Chelton and Dorothy Broderick of the American Library Association, who provided support, clippings, and books, and to my family, who put up with my dazed preoccupation during the many months this book was in preparation.

# 1

# *What Every Young Man Should Know*

"What every young man should know" is a piece of American folk-lore, a phrase that evokes earnest but irrelevant mini-instruction in sex, a mythical title whose mention evokes snickers and knowing leers. Was there ever actually such a book? Did it deserve the snickers and leers with which it has been remembered? Was this proto-type of American sex education a reality?

Not only did it exist, it existed in six editions and eleven trans-lations. It had seven companion volumes that provided sex instruc-tion for both sexes from cradle to grave. It was much admired, widely read, and although it was not the first of its genre, it set the tone for the sex education of teenagers for fifty years. The many chap-ters of elementary biology, tracing the reproductive process from the simplest forms of life up to mammals, are remembered as "the birds and the bees"—a phrase that became a common metaphor for embar-rassed and clumsy attempts to communicate the facts of life. But most of all, the book is characterized by its hortatory tone, its dire warnings and deliberate avoidance of the urgent questions of the young—features of most sex education books for teenagers up until nearly the present day.

The title behind the myth was actually *What a Young Boy Ought to Know*, which the folk memory, with its own aesthetics, has round-ed off to the more rhythmic "What every young man should know." It was written by Sylvanus Stall, a retired Lutheran minister with an astute business sense (one of his first books was *How to Pay Church Debts, and How to Keep Churches Out of Debt*). In his new career as a sex educator, or "purity advocate," Stall put his clerical background and business savvy to good use. With the success of *Young Boy*, Stall

1

almost immediately launched the more ambitious project of producing a series of age-oriented advice manuals based on the format of
*What a Young Boy Ought to Know.* In the same year in which *Young
Boy* was published, Stall wrote a sequel for older teens, *What a
Young Man Ought to Know,* and a third book, for the newly married
male, *What a Young Husband Ought to Know.* Turning to the market
for the other half of the human race, he contracted with Dr. Mary
Wood-Allen to write companion volumes for girls and women. In
1897 she wrote *What a Young Girl Ought to Know* and the next year
turned out *What a Young Woman Ought to Know.* Rounding out the
series in the three years, Stall added *What a Man of Forty-five Ought
to Know* (1901) and asked another woman doctor, Emma F. Drake, to
write *What a Young Wife Ought to Know* (1901) and *What a Woman
of Forty-five Ought to Know* (1902).

These eight books were marketed as the Self and Sex series; "Purity and Truth" is embossed on the cover and heads the title page. A
portrait of the author in clerical collar appears on the frontispiece,
and shows a neatly combed man with a modest beard and kindly
eyes behind gold-rimmed spectacles. The series was heavily promoted under the slogan "Pure books on avoided subjects." Every volume
bears copious advertisements for the others in the series, some even
including facsimile pages of translations into French, German, Span-
ish, Dutch, Swedish, Japanese, Korean, Hindi, Bengali, Telugu, and
Persian-Urdu. In 1907, Stall wrote a guidebook for his sales staff,
entitled *Successful Selling of the Self and Sex Series.*

Each book opens with a dozen pages of "Commendations from
Eminent Men and Women," including citations from officers of the
American Purity Alliance, the Society for Moral and Sanitary Prophylaxis, and the Women's Christian Temperance Union, as well as
a number of prominent clergymen and evangelists. Accompanying
the citations are a series of stiff portraits depicting grim-visaged figures in high collars or muttonchops whiskers. Ironically, early editions included a commendation from Anthony Comstock, solicitor
of the U.S. Post Office and sponsor of the prudish obscenity laws that
were to hinder American sex education until 1971. Although this
impressive gallery warded off any suspicion of lasciviousness or
erotic intent on the part of the authors or publisher, the medical authorities were cautious in their approval. In 1901 this reserved recommendation from the *Journal of the American Medical
Association* appeared in advertisements for the series: "We find
nothing from which to dissent, but much to commend."

The format of *What a Young Boy Ought to Know* is a series of chats supposedly recorded on cylinders (audiovisual instruction was modish even in 1897) for a young teenager named Harry. Harry has asked, on the occasion of the birth of a baby sister, "Where do babies come from?" A friend of the family has been asked to instruct him, and has recorded these talks "to take the place of his dear mama's nightly visits to the nursery" while she is busy with the new baby.

The first chapters are a heavily theological description of "God's purpose in endowing plants, animals, and man with reproductive organs." We hear about Adam and Eve as the first parents, "father, mother, and baby plants," and "the early life of the baby oyster." At the end of Part I, the mechanics of human reproduction are dispensed with in one sentence: "God has ordained that the ovum, while yet in the body of the wife, shall be fertilized by the requisite and proper bodily contact of the husband." Part II warns against masturbation—"the manner in which the reproductive organs are injured in boys by abuse." Harry is told about "God's purpose in giving us hands" (or rather, what is not God's purpose in giving us hands). He learns that "some boys weaken and disease their bodies by developing an unnatural appetite for vinegar, salt, cloves, coffee, slate pencils. . . ." Such habits diminish a boy's ability to resist temptation and may lead to the practice of secret and social vice. "Words are scarcely capable," thunders the author, "of describing the dreadful consequences which are suffered by those who persist in this practise." Self-abuse causes suffering for the boy's parents and sister, his children may be born in poverty, his offspring will be inferior because he has "injured his reproductive powers." The practice leads to "idiocy, and even death." His mind fails, his health declines, and early death ensues. "Boys often have to be put in a straitjacket or their hands tied to the bedposts or to rings in the wall." A boy who secretly indulges in this vice develops a shifty glance and "pulls his cap down so as to hide his eyes" when passing people in the street. The closing chapters admonish boys to recover their purity through self-control and to help their comrades do the same. "It is our duty to aid others to avoid pernicious habits and to retain or regain their purity and strength."

As strange as this book may seem to us today, the views it expresses were solidly rooted in the accepted beliefs of the time. In particular, Stall's diatribe against masturbation offers significant clues to the Victorian concept of the nature of sexuality and begins to suggest why sex education books for young people began to appear almost explosively at that time in history.

## Self-Control in Victorian Sexuality

Lack of restraint in sexual matters was seen throughout much of the nineteenth century as not only morally wrong but also physically and socially harmful. A metaphor that came to be accepted by the late Victorians as scientific fact was the idea that a man's physical, mental, and spiritual health depended upon the retention of semen within the body. Conversely, loss of semen was interpreted as a loss of the essence of vitality. In an unpublished paper titled "The Origins of Sex Education in America 1890–1920: An Inquiry into Victorian Sexuality," Bryan Strong explores how this pseudoscientific theory was used to explain the need to suppress sexuality:

> This theory, which possessed remarkable similarities to Freud's theory of sublimation, was a materialistic explanation of biological and intellectual growth. It stated essentially that the testes, "through some hidden and not yet understood process slowly secreted cells" within the semen which, if the semen were not expended, were absorbed by the blood. The absorption of these cells enabled the young male to develop his body, let his voice become masculine, and grow a full beard. If the physically mature man refrained from sexual excesses and remained continent, then the semen was absorbed by the blood and was carried to the brain where it was "coined into new thoughts—perhaps new inventions—grand conceptions of the true, the beautiful, the useful, or into fresh emotions of joy and impulses of kindness." This explanation, however much disguised as science, in reality reflected Victorian morality since its actual function was to offer positive rewards for sexual repression.

As Strong further explains, the Victorians believed that man's sexual behavior was the model and source for the rest of his character; the habits of restraint developed in that area led to the acquisition of "the Victorian constellation of values which included work, industry, good habits, piety, and noble ideals. Indeed, without sexual repression the Victorians believed that it was impossible for those other values to exist in an ideal character. If a man were pure, he was also frugal, hard working, temperate, and governed by habit. If, on the other hand, he were impure, he was also a spend-thrift, disposed to speculation, whisky-drinking, and ruled by his impulses."

By expending his seminal power in illicit intercourse, masturbation, lewd thoughts leading to nocturnal emissions, or even excesses in the marriage bed, a man would damage his health drastically. He would waste away, become pale, hollow-cheeked, and silly. He might contract venereal disease, develop "spermatorrhea" (a chronic and involuntary loss of semen), or go insane; his business might fail and he would surely die an early death. Charles Scudder, in *Handbook for Young Men*, phrased this idea succinctly in 1892: "Bodily vigor and moral integrity depend on personal purity. This great force curbed and restrained, expends itself in the business of life and makes a man useful and successful."

Purity and self-restraint were equally important within the marriage bond. A husband's responsibility to maintain his own health and purity was inextricably bound with his obligation to his family, which resulted in a curious bifurcation of the sexual impulse. Although the restrained expression of sex within marriage was holy and spiritual (the family was the cornerstone of Victorian society and the center of a woman's life as wife and mother), uncontrolled sex between married couples was physical and base. If a man were impure, his wife's health could be ruined by contact with him.

Furthermore, because the Victorians subscribed to Lamarckian theories of heredity, they also believed that the presumed effects of sexual misconduct could be passed on to one's offspring in the form of tendencies toward dissipation.

Thus, the vehemence of Stall's argument against masturbation in *What a Young Boy Ought to Know* is typical of Victorian pleas for self-restraint. The purity advocates were most especially concerned that young people should not learn "solitary vice." It was not only the significance they attached to the loss of semen, however, that inspired such strong emotions in addressing the young. The masturbatory act is done solely for pleasure: it can be carried on in secret and is easily hidden from parents; and, most important, it sets a pattern for adult sexual attitudes. A teenager who masturbates is finding out that sex feels good, a very dangerous piece of knowledge by Victorian standards. On the other hand, a boy who can be taught to look on his own genitals and their needs with loathing and fear has been taught to repress sexuality all his life.

Ronald Walters, in *Primers for Prudery*, an excellent survey of mid-Victorian sexual attitudes, carries this explanation even further: "The authorities continually harped on masturbation's supposedly self-destructive nature: it was self-abuse and self-pollution. There could scarcely be a more straightforward way of representing sex as a personal impulse with which each human being (including authors of advice manuals, presumably) must struggle. Concern for masturbation, then, easily became a screen upon which to project one's own unconscious battle with drives that orthodox morality demanded be subjugated." Walters also points out that concern about masturbation increased as changes in nineteenth-century society created new opportunities for privacy and solitary indulgence. Such social factors included "the isolation experienced by new arrivals to urban areas, simultaneous production of larger homes and smaller families, the growth of boarding schools, [and the] increasing removal of middle-class children from the workday world of adults."

The clarion call to parents to face the task of instructing the young in the heretofore unmentionable facts of life was being issued as early as the 1880s, around the same time that antimasturbation pamphlets for young men had begun to appear. During most of the Victorian era the accepted method of sex education had been deliberate silence, but now parents were becoming increasingly concerned that their children would acquire bad habits from their peers if they were not carefully supervised and provided with the armor of "right knowledge." ("Ignorance is vice," erroneously attributed to Plato, appears on the title page of *What a Young Boy Ought to Know.*)

George Franklin Hall, in an 1892 book titled *Plain Points on Personal Purity, or Startling Sins of the Sterner Sex*, lists signs of self-abuse to alert parents to their sons' possible debauchery. Adults were to watch for any or all of the following: change in character (from cheerful, obedient, energetic to irritable, sullen, stupid, reticent); decline in health; precocious development ("a senile look") or deficiency in development; unnatural lassitude, especially in the morning; love of being alone; shyness or boldness (to hide inability to look a person in the eye); strange appetites for clay, chalk, and slate pencils; use of tobacco; round shoulders; an unnaturally stiff, wriggling gait; twitching; a decided preference for the society of little girls; pain in the back, headache, full veins, bedwetting, palpitations, pimples (especially on the forehead), epilepsy, or wet palms, abnormal development or underdevelopment of the parts; and stains on underclothing or bedding.

Once detected, however, a wayward boy should not be made to feel that all hope is lost, warns Hall. Lest he become discouraged at seeking salvation and sink into a slough of self-gratification, the youth should be reassured that the effects of masturbation are almost entirely reversible for those who learn self-mastery. As we shall see, Hall and his contemporaries provide a variety of techniques for developing the requisite mastery, ranging from hymn singing to sitting in a bowl of ice water.

Published by the White Cross Committee of the Young Men's

Christian Association, a group pledged to the promotion of purity, Scudder's *Hand-book for Young Men* also appeared in 1892. Despite the title, the book is addressed to parents and other sex educators. The tone of righteousness and missionary purpose is immediately apparent in the opening paragraphs: "The light of knowledge must be shed abroad in larger measure, in order to drive away the darkness. This book has been prepared to arm the advocates of purity with arguments wherewith to meet their adversaries." Scudder expounds at length on the necessity for conserving seminal power, the theme that was to appear regularly for the next forty years, and ends on a note of patriotism: "So we conclude our short work with a purely American question addressed to each reader. Does impurity pay? If not, then join your heart, mind and soul with ours to fight down this hideous vice, and let us all unite in a determined effort to be pure ourselves, to esteem the purity of woman, and to uphold the pure honor of America! "

## A New Genre

The years between 1892 and 1920 saw the publication of several dozen sex education tracts addressed to adolescents themselves. Advice manuals for married people and for youth in their twenties had already become plentiful by this time, but the book meant for the teenager's own reading was an innovation. Indeed, the very idea of "teenage" is a Victorian invention, as Walters reminds us: "Nineteenth century writers also fashioned the concept of adolescence, an idea we take for granted although it is actually of comparatively recent origin (previous generations simply expected youth to assume adult duties at a far younger age than at present). Cautionary literature, with its continual fretting about resisting sexual activity in the decade or more between puberty and marriage, encouraged people to regard these years as a special time with special problems (including sexual ones). . . ."

Why was it that sex education books for the young appeared so suddenly and in such quantity at the turn of the century? The ideas they expounded had been generally accepted for most of the nineteenth century, but in the late Victorian era the signs of a disintegration of the old social order, such as those mentioned by Walters in regard to the increased isolation of the individual, aroused an urgency about preserving the sexual attitudes that had been one of its foundations. As the Industrial Revolution grew in

America, the work ethic of frugality and self-denial began to give way to an ethic of consumption and self-indulgence as the American economy matured. This was inevitably reflected in a loosening of regard for accepted sexual attitudes. New scientific research led to a more realistic understanding of the mechanics of sex—the functioning of the union of the sperm and the ovum, for instance, was discovered in 1875. From the other side of the Atlantic the early works of Freud, Shaw, and Havelock Ellis were challenging accepted sexual ideas. (Although the first title of Ellis' monumental *Studies in the Psychology of Sex* was published in England in 1897, the complete seven-volume work was available in the United States only to the medical profession until 1935.)

These and other advocates of sex as pleasure (the free lovers of the Oneida Community, for example, who practiced group marriage) panicked the American late Victorians into energetic attempts to indoctrinate the young. The very core of their civilization was challenged. Having long ago eschewed the more relaxed attitudes of the eighteenth and early nineteenth centuries, the late Victorians were convinced that sexual restraint was essential to the development of the individual and the progress of society. Ignoring the lessons of history regarding what Walters has called "cycles of frankness," they now prepared to do battle with the return of that cycle in the twentieth century.

Thus, with the covergence of all these social, psychological, and historical factors, a new literary genre, the sex education book for young adults, emerged. The first true example of the genre that appears in the comprehensive subject catalog of the Kinsey Institute for Sex Research is *Confidential Talks with Young Men* (1892) by Lyman Beecher Sperry, which will be examined in some detail later in this chapter. Other early examples predating the Self and Sex Series are *Almost a Man* (1895) by Mary Wood-Allen, also to be examined in this chapter, and the companion volumes for girls, *Confidential Talks with Young Women* (1893) by Sperry and *Almost a Woman* (1897) by Wood-Allen, discussed in Chapter 2. The primary purpose of all these early works was to provide just enough anatomical explanation to blunt the curiosity of the young so that they would not seek information from their contemporaries, and to warn them away from any sexual thoughts, feelings, or actions.

## Stall and Predecessors

Stall's second book for the Self and Sex series, *What a Young Man Ought to Know* (1897), is a predictable product of the foregoing purposes and beliefs. Written for men in their late teens and early twenties, it begins with praise for the value of physical strength, which, of course, results from sexual self-mastery. Stall warns that, although lack of personal purity (secret vice) can lead to unmanly weakness, as well as many other horrid conditions, losses of the seminal fluids in sleep are not necessarily abnormal. (Obsessed as they were with sexual control, the Victorians apparently found the prospect of involuntary loss of semen, even in sleep, alarming.) In any case, young men should be aware of the dangers of consulting quacks and charlatans and seek advice only from reputable physicians.

Alarmed at the ignorance concerning the diseases that accompany vice, Stall presents a lurid picture of the symptoms and complications of gonorrhea and syphilis. He describes how healthy brides become early and permanent invalids, and asks (without much hope) "Can it ever by cured?" A chapter on the reproductive organs follows, with some cautionary words on their purpose and their willful debasement. Marriage is a great blessing, he urges, but unbridled sexuality even within that institution can cause great unhappiness. In conclusion, a man should get all the help he can for self-mastery by the right choice of companions, books, pictures, and recreation. He should eschew liquor and tobacco, rise early, and adopt habits of industry. He should rely on the influence of an ennobling affection and, most of all, honor the Sabbath, the church, and the Bible.

Of the other Self and Sex titles for boys and men, *What a Young Husband Ought to Know* (1897) first warns against sexual excesses in marriage and the miseries visited on a marriage by vice in earlier years, and then discusses the nature of woman ("God has fitted her for her sphere") and the joys of parenthood and the family. *What a Man of Forty-five Ought to Know* (1901) is that at that age he should enter in a "sexual hush" and prepare himself for some strange behavior from his wife as she goes into menopause. A description of the physical changes and mental manifestations of menopause follows and the book ends with some cheering words on the "character of hospitals on mental sickness." The four titles for females by Emma Drake and Mary Wood-Allen will be discussed in the next chapter.

Let us look now at Stall's predecessors. Although *What a Young Boy Ought to Know* was the first book of its kind to win wide acceptance, a much more informative work had been published five years earlier in 1892—*Confidential Talks with Young Men* by Lyman Beecher Sperry (the companion volume, *Confidential Talks with Young Women*, was written by Sperry a year later), A comparison of Stall's and Sperry's books suggests that *Confidential Talks with*

*Young Men* may have provided the pattern for the early chapters of *Young Boy.* Sperry was a "lecturer on Sanitary Science at Carleton College" and a physician. The straightforward and unornamented style of his book and the knowledgeable descriptions of anatomy and sexual acts he includes indicate a man of science accustomed to dealing with matters of fact. Sperry also reveals a sense of admiration and wonder for the intricacies of nature that sometimes emerges in un-Victorian metaphors, such as "Flowers are the sex organs of plants." He evidently felt no need for the theological justification and bombast that Stall later employed, although Sperry was no less devoted to the promotion of purity.

*Confidential Talks with Young Men* opens with an introduction addressed to parents. Explaining the newly felt need for sex education, he urges parents, teachers, and physicians to teach the facts of sex so the young will not get "venomous ideas from corrupt playmates." Although knowledge is not a guarantee of pure living, it is far safer than ignorance or distorted and poisoned notions. There is no hope of raising boys in ignorance of sex; the world has tried it for centuries and failed, says Sperry, adding that since only 5 percent of American youth attend church regularly, there is also little hope for help from that quarter. The problem is serious: "Lust can truthfully claim more victims than tobacco even" and it is "the most common and most serious vice of youth." Explaining the importance to society of training in sexual control, Sperry points to "the far-reaching power of the reproductive system over every other organ and function," and declares that "vigor of body, strength of mind, and integrity of moral character depend largely on personal purity [and] on the proper development and use of the reproductive organs." Youths who indulge in unrestrained sex become defective specimens, capable of transmitting not only "venereal disease and taints" but feeble bodies, unbalanced minds, and lustful tendencies.

After this introduction, the book itself is addressed to boys in their midteens. The early chapters, as imitated by Stall, deal with the reproductive arrangements of various forms of life on an ascending scale of complexity. First he describes reproduction of plants, followed by "the multiplication of oysters and fishes," "the propagation of insects and birds," "the perpetuation of marsupials and mammals," and last, human reproduction. Here Sperry is at great pains to explain the differences between the male urinary and reproductive systems. A most peculiar diagram appears as illustration: all of the major parts of the genital and urinary anatomy are labeled and described, including the penis and the testicles, but the latter two items do not appear in the drawing. Where they should be are only blank spaces with identifying numerals.

In the next chapter Sperry arrives at a vital subject: puberty and self-abuse. Sperry stresses the contrasts between the gelding and the stallion, the capon and the rooster, to show the benefits of proper masculine development. Since he, like his contemporaries, is convinced that this development depends on the body's reabsorption of sperm, the argument moves quite logically to an indictment of masturbation. He describes this act with surprising accuracy: "an artificial excitement of the penis sufficient to produce an erection and lustful desires terminating in a spasm of the sexual organ which, in those who are sufficiently developed, produces an emission of semen." Noting that "artificial excitement" may be achieved by imagination alone, inflamed by lustful thoughts, lewd reading, or indecent pictures, Sperry cautions that this is equally as harmful as manual manipulation. For the most part, however, Sperry is cheerfully humanistic in emphasizing the healthy development of the reproductive system, although he mentions the "harvest of horrible conditions" reaped by the masturbator. Unlike Stall, he mercifully refrains from enumerating them.

Sperry then broaches the problem of nocturnal emissions, a source of considerable anxiety to male Victorians. Sperry hastens to reassure the reader that nocturnal emissions are normal and natural. Frequent emissions may sometimes cause debility, but far more often the reverse is true—a weakened condition of the body leads to increased ejaculation. On the whole, it would be better if semen were absorbed as produced "to spare the nervous system the shock of emission," but "in some cases . . . emissions really seem to clear up the brain and increase the sensation of bodily vigor."

Unnatural emissions, however, are another matter completely. Sperry advises readers to be alert to signs of spermatorrhea, and passes on the widely accepted belief that this condition, "sad to contemplate and terrible to experience," can be caused by physical or mental self-abuse. However, spermatorrhea is not as common as many suppose, comforts Sperry.

For those young men who are worried by too frequent emissions, Sperry provides what was to become staple antimasturbation advice—a list of practical remedies. First, he says, indulge in no lustful thoughts; crowd them out by thinking of your mother's pure love, reading the Sermon on the Mount, praying for help, or singing a soul-stirring hymn. Eat a nonstimulating diet (avoid meat and eggs, pepper, mustard, spices); and avoid tea, coffee, alcohol, and tobacco.

Choose physical labor in the open air instead of mental work. Get plenty of sleep and arise immediately on waking. Bathe often (but not every day). Seek the company of sensible women, and quit worrying about sexual matters.

Predictably, Sperry uses the chapter on prostitution to demolish the myth of "sexual necessity" (the belief that a sexual outlet is needed for health) and to catalog the horrors of venereal disease. But he also takes the position that a male who visits a lady of the evening is as degraded as she—"a just human judgement will stamp the word prostitute on the one as surely as on the other." He estimates that one-third of the population of civilized countries has, or will have, venereal disease, and heightens the impact of this alarming statistic by providing vivid descriptions of the primary and secondary symptoms of "venereal ulcers—the Almighty's 'registered stamp' for the act of adultery." He attacks the rationalization, still heard today, that "gonorrhea is no more troublesome than a bad cold." Sperry warns that venereal disease can be transmitted by kissing (a common Victorian warning) but explains that the receiving party must have an open sore on the mouth (an uncommon clarification of that warning). He mentions no cure.

Next, Sperry discourses eloquently on the evil of quackery. The intense sexual repressions and anxieties of young men must have made them easy prey for clever advertisements that played on their fears and ignorance. Newspapers were thick with ads by "experienced physicians" or "returned missionaries" promising to cure, for large sums of money, vaguely described sexual ills that might otherwise prove fatal. Lacking basic knowledge of their bodies' sexual functions, young men could easily be persuaded by the unscrupulous that even normal responses like nocturnal emissions were symptoms of disease. In this vacuum of ignorance, any explanation was seized upon.

Sperry describes one of the forms of quackery that exploited this hunger for information—the "Museum of Anatomy." These shows (for men only) were free or charged only ten cents. On entering, the boys and men were treated to the sight of a nude reclining female figure in wax, usually copied from a famous painting. Proceeding with passions aroused, they viewed scenes of the horrors of the Inquisition or historical battles (the traditional duo of sex and violence). Next came lurid and exaggerated representations of the dreadful results of venereal disease, self-abuse, and other sexual excesses. As the trembling victim emerged, he was handed a pamphlet advertising a quack whose offices were nearby and who was available right then for consultation.

Sperry ends his book with a section of sensible advice on healthful living. He especially deplores the use of tobacco (an opinion that must have been amusing to readers in the first half of the century, but now, ironically, we find ourselves nodding in agreement). It is interesting to notice what Sperry does *not* include. There is no mention of normal human sexual intercourse, nor is there any talk of courting or marriage or the family. Sperry's only discussion of the relationship between the sexes is in reference to prostitution. Still, *Confidential Talks with Young Men* is extraordinarily candid for its time, and deserved better than the oblivion it received.

Another forerunner of the Self and Sex series was *Almost a Man* by Mary Wood-Allen, M.D., first published in 1895. Evidently it was this volume and its counterpart, *Almost a Woman* (1897), that brought Wood-Allen to the attention of Sylvanus Stall when he was casting about for someone with prestige and experience to write the volumes for women of his series. Wood-Allen was not shy about sex education; in 1892 she had written a booklet on the subject titled *Teaching Truth* ("Its sweet truth is like the breath of a May morning" claimed an advertisement), which was later expanded to become the flagship of the Teaching Truth series. And in 1895 she had written a treatise for lay people on human physiology, a very daring project for a woman, even if she was a doctor. This work had the cumbersome title *The Marvels of Our Bodily Dwelling; Physiology Made Interesting; Suitable as a Text-book or Reference Book in Schools, or for Pleasant Home Reading*. Some, but not all, of the editions of 1895 cautiously added a sixteen-page supplementary chapter, "The Birthchamber," which was also published separately as a pamphlet.

But it was the pseudo-fiction, *Almost a Man*, that most clearly showed Wood-Allen's devotion to the cause of purity. With its skeletal plot and didactic tone, this book could be called the first young adult junior novel. Certainly it has all the earmarks of the genre that was developed in the 1950s by writers such as Jeannette Eyerly and Betty Cavanna, including the awkward attempt to use current teenage speech patterns, the depiction of an all-wise adult who advises the young person, and the transparent manipulation of plot to make a moral point.

As the book opens, four young boys—Guy, Frank, Carl, and Rob—are lolling about by a stream in a field, discussing how boring life is at home and how much fun it would be to run away. The author hints that one or two of the boys may have a more serious reason than boredom for wanting a change of scene—Guy, for instance, has a tendency to pull his cap down over his eyes. Along the road comes Dr. Lynn with her satchel and, seeing the boys up to no good, she crosses the field and sits down with them on a log. After a bit of conversation, she senses the problems on their minds, and invites them to come to her house the next week, with their parents' permission, to be told the facts of life. The boys are delighted, and rush off to get the requisite parental consent.

A few days later, Guy, cap in hand, appears on the doctor's doorstep. He has not been able to wait until the meeting to talk about his problem, and besides, he doesn't want the other fellows to know about it. Guy, as the reader has been led to suspect, is a self-abuser. He confesses his vice to Dr. Lynn, but she is not a bit shocked. Instead, she gives him a pat on the back and some practical advice. Overcoming this evil practice takes willpower and he must train like an athlete to succeed, the doctor begins. Guy must give up tea and coffee, keep his bowels open, sleep on a hard bed, and get up the minute he wakes. And before retiring he must take a cold bath and then sit in a bowl of cold water. Dr. Lynn's encouraging words hearten Guy, and he goes away confident in his ability to conquer himself.

On the agreed-upon day, the boys assemble at Dr. Lynn's house. She begins by assuring them that sex is beautiful and the basis of human life. Then comes a short version of the birds and the bees—explanations of plant and animal reproduction, stopping short of human beings. Dr. Lynn passes around a generous supply of a temperance and antimasturbation tract entitled "A Gateway and a Gift, written for the Land of Teens" and impresses the boys with the Victorian misconception that behavior influences heredity: "You can change yourself by education so that the inheritance of your children may be quite changed." After a few more discreet words on solitary vice, the doctor hands around copies of the "White Cross Pledge" (sponsored by the same organization of the Young Men's Christian Association that had published Charles Scudder's *Hand-book for Young Men*) for the boys to sign. This pledge, headed by the motto "Blessed are the pure in heart: for they shall see God," provides an interesting summary of the guiding laws of purity:

I PROMISE, BY THE HELP OF GOD:
1. To treat all women with respect, and endeavor to protect them from wrong and degradation;
2. To endeavor to put down all indecent language and coarse jests;
3. To maintain the law of purity as equally binding upon men and women;
4. To endeavor to spread these principles among my companions, and to try to help my younger brothers;
5. To use all possible means to fulfill the command "Keep thyself pure."

A few days later the doctor again has a visitor. This time it is Frank who has the problem. In a panic over something strange that had happened to him (we gather that he means nocturnal emissions), he noticed an advertisement that promised help for his "ailment." Hopeful, he sent for advice and medicine, which didn't help. Now he has received a bill for $20—a huge sum in an age when $10 a week was a living wage. Dr. Lynn assures him of his normalcy (but doesn't tell him what to do about the bill).

When the boys again visit Dr. Lynn, she has had time to suspect that their problems are caused by idle hands. Suddenly she has an idea. Her attic is not being used, and there are some carpenter's tools up there; they will form a manual arts workshop club. Her enthusiasm carries the project through, and she also helps to set up a manual arts program in the schools. The clubroom is also outfitted with Indian clubs and other exercise equipment and a library (which gives an excuse to end the book with a list of good reading for boys).

Despite its obvious contrivances, *Almost a Man* tried to meet young people on their own level, instead of thundering at them from the pulpit. There is almost no factual content, of course, and a boy who was ignorant about masturbation or nocturnal emissions would learn nothing here except that the former was forbidden and the latter was normal. Coitus, as might be expected, is never mentioned. Still, Wood-Allen's warmth and kindness must have been some comfort to Victorian boys, who were faced with sexual warnings and horrors in every direction.

## BIBLIOGRAPHY

Drake, Emma Frances. *What a Woman of Forty-five Ought to Know*. Self and Sex Series. Philadelphia: Vir Publishing Co., 1902.

———. *What a Young Wife Ought to Know*. Self and Sex Series. Philadelphia: Vir Publishing Co., 1901.

Hall, George F. *Plain Points on Personal Purity, or Startling Sins of the Sterner Sex*. Chicago: Columbian Book Co., 1892.

Scudder, Charles D. *Hand-book for Young Men*. New York: White Cross Committee, Young Men's Christian Association of the City of New York, 1892.

Sperry, Lyman Beecher. *Confidential Talks with Young Men*. Chicago: Fleming H. Revell Co., 1892.

———. *Confidential Talks with Young Women*. Chicago: Fleming H. Revell Co., 1893.

Stall, Sylvanus. *How to Pay Church Debts, and How to Keep Churches Out of Debt*. New York: I. K. Funk and Co., 1881.

————. *Successful Selling of the Self and Sex Series*. Philadelphia: Vir Publishing Co., 1907.

————. *What a Man of Forty-five Ought to Know*. Self and Sex Series. Philadelphia: Vir Publishing Co., 1901.

————. *What a Young Boy Ought to Know*. Self and Sex Series. Philadephia: Vir Publishing Co., 1897; rev. eds., 1905, 1909.

————. *What a Young Husband Ought to Know*. Self and Sex Series. Philadelphia: Vir Publishing Co., 1897; rev. ed., 1907.

————. *What a Young Man Ought to Know*. Self and Sex Series. Philadelphia: Vir Publishing Co., 1897; rev. ed., 1904.

Strong, Bryan. "The Origins of Sex Education in America 1890–1920: An Inquiry into Victorian Sexuality." Located in library of the Institute for Sex Research, Indiana University, n.d.

Walters, Ronald G. *Primers for Prudery: Sexual Advice to Victorian America*. Englewood Cliffs, NJ: Prentice-Hall, 1974.

Wood-Allen, Mary. *Almost a Man*. Ann Arbor, MI: Wood-Allen Publishing Co., 1895.

————. *Almost a Woman*. Ann Arbor, MI: Wood-Allen Publishing Co., 1897.

————. *The Marvels of Our Bodily Dwelling; Physiology Made Interesting; Suitable as a Text-book or Reference Book in Schools, or for Pleasant Home Reading*. With supplementary chapter "The Birthchamber." Ann Arbor, MI: Wood-Allen Publishing Co., 1895.

————. *Teaching Truth*. Ann Arbor, MI: Wood-Allen Publishing Co., 1892.

————. *Teaching Truth*. Teaching Truth Series. Ann Arbor, MI: Wood-Allen Publishing Co., 1903.

————. *What a Young Girl Ought to Know*. Self and Sex Series. Philadephia: Vir Publishing Co., 1897.

————. *What a Young Woman Ought to Know*. Self and Sex Series. Philadelphia: Vir Publishing Co., 1898.

# 2

# *What Every Young Girl Should Know*

In 1887 Dr. J. W. Howe, an eminent physician, wrote *Excessive Venery, Masturbation, and Continence.* His subject was the curing of the "disease" of masturbation. In Chapter 6 he mentions in passing that the appropriate medical treatment for young girls who show excessive sexual interest is amputation of the clitoris. An appalling theory, but even more appalling is the fact Howe was professor of clinical surgery at Bellevue Hospital Medical College in New York City, and very likely had many opportunities to put his theories into practice.

Howe's ideas were not universally accepted, but they are symptomatic of the Victorian attitude toward feminine sexuality. A woman who showed erotic feelings was perceived as demented, diseased, or evil, and sometimes all three. The ideal Victorian lady was delicate, refined, and pure. Her nature was defined in terms of her role as "the angel in the house" who ministered to the spiritual and physical needs of the family. Her sexuality was acknowledged only in connection with the exalted function of childbearing and thus, in a way, transcended sex. The purpose of sex education for a girl, then, was to prepare her for the demands of motherhood and impress her with the grave moral and spiritual responsibilities of the role. She was given just enough information about her own body so that she could stay healthy, care for herself during menstruation, and preserve her virtue from evils that were never really explained to her. The books of this period constantly return to the refrain of the sacred joys of motherhood—the ultimate purpose of a girl's existence.

There were a number of changes afoot in the woman's sphere at the turn of the century that made the late Victorians feel the need to reinforce this rigidly defined feminine role. The first women's rights convention had been held in 1848 in Seneca Falls, and from it emerged a vocal feminist leadership. Agitation for women's suffrage had begun, and in England would soon lead to demonstrations and arrests. Higher education for women was becoming accepted—Vassar, Smith, Wellesley, and Barnard were building fine academic reputations.

Male writers rose to these challenges with ridicule and condemnation for the "new woman," often disguised as praise for the fair sex in general. In 1895 Charles H. Parkhurst wrote a volume of essays, *Talks to Young Women*, which refers to women who demand equal rights as "andromaniacs" and stresses woman's mission of motherhood: "Nature has so wrought its opinions into the tissue of woman's physical constitution and function that any feminine attempt to mutiny against wifehood, motherhood, and domestic 'limitations' is a hopeless and rather imbecile attempt to escape the inevitable. . . . A true mother lives for her children, and knows no other ambition but to live in her children." He approves the idea of college for women ("It is one of the pleasant features of our generation that increased attention is being given to the discipline of the female mind"), but only if that education is used for motherhood ("There is no 'strong-mindedness' and no completeness of college training that will unsex her, provided only such possessions and acquisitions are dominated by the feminine instinct and mortgaged to maternal ends and purposes"). Suffrage for women will get his reluctant sanction only when women have exhausted the opportunities for excelling in their own sphere: "I have not even uttered a word against so serious an innovation as that of woman's going to the polls. I have only tried to show the infinite stretch of opportunity that opens before her in the line of service which the general instinct and the revealed word of God show to be primarily pertinent to her. When the sex has succeeded in doing perfectly what God and nature evidently intended to have her do, it will be ample time for her to think about doing some things upon which God and nature have expressed themselves less definitely."

In *Steps up Life's Ladder* (1905), a book of inspirational essays for teenage boys, Charles A. Ingraham took Parkhurst's idea of andromania to its logical conclusion—women who broke through the accepted boundaries of feminine behavior had ceased to be women and had defined themselves as male: "The girls of masculine proclivities can hardly be admitted into the decorous circle of elect maidens. They may succeed in stunning the corner loungers with the exhibition of their horsemanship and the mannish cut of their coats; they may be able to converse intelligently and fluently on political topics; they may have the capacity to buy and sell and make money; but, after all, what the world wants of a girl is to be a girl, not a tom-boy."

This was the social setting, then, in which Mary Wood-Allen was asked to write *What a Young Girl Ought to Know* in 1897. Who was Mary Wood-Allen? What kind of a woman did Sylvanus Stall select to join in his profitable sex education enterprise? The frontispiece photograph in *Young Girl* and *Young Woman* shows her as sweet-faced and a bit plump, in a lacy collar and brooch, and with wavy hair pulled back into a bun from a high, rounded forehead. From all the evidence, she was a person with considerable strength and independence of thought. She was a medical doctor at a time when that degree was a difficult accomplishment for a woman; she wrote prolifically on subjects that were previously taboo for women writers; and she published her early works herself under the imprint "Wood-Allen Publishing Company." Her maiden name was Wood and her married name Allen; the hyphenated Wood-Allen must have been a statement of identity for her. (The Library of Congress and most other U.S. libraries have robbed her of that statement, however, by entering her books in the files under "Allen, Mary [Wood]" in strict adherence to *Anglo-American Cataloging Rules*.) After her reputation as a sex educator was established by the Self and Sex series, she was offered, and accepted, the post of World Superintendent of the Purity Department of the Women's Christian Temperance Union.

Wood-Allen's first books were the Teaching Truth series ("Treats of the instruction to be given the young regarding sex and parenthood"), which she at first published herself, beginning with *Teaching Truth* in 1892. *Almost a Man* and *Almost a Woman* were early titles in this series; later titles included *Child-Confidence Rewarded* and *Caring for the Baby*. Another series launched by Wood-Allen was the American Motherhood leaflets. These dealt with family relations, and had such titles as *Keep Mother and Me Intimate*, *Adolescence*, and *A Noble Father*. Her physiology text, *The Marvels of Our Bodily Dwelling* (first published in 1895), was popular for years and was published in five editions, the last appearing in 1915. In 1901, after the success of *What a Young Girl Ought to Know*, she tried her hand at marital advice with *Ideal Married Life: A Book for All Husbands and Wives* (could it be that she felt slighted by Stall's choice of Emma Drake to write the Self and Sex volumes for adult women?). Wood-Allen continued to write on family living and sex education until her death in 1908. A posthumous collection of her works, *Making the Best of Our Children* (1909), was edited by her daughter, Rose

Woodallen Chapman, who was herself a well-known sex educator and columnist for the *Ladies' Home Journal*.

## Preparing for Motherhood

Like all the books in the Self and Sex series, *What a Young Girl Ought to Know* opens with a formidable battery of "Commendations from Eminent Men and Women." Wood-Allen's choice of members in these galleries is revealing, not only of Victorian standards of prestige but also of the author's changing patterns of friendships and alliances. For *Young Girl* the eminent women are representative of causes and professions closely connected to the purity movement. Included are the national and international presidents of the Women's Christian Temperance Union, the president of the National Christian League for the Promotion of Social Purity, and one or two minor authors of works on domestic arrangements ("The Model Nursery," "House and Domestic Decorations"). Among the eminent men cited are the physical director of the Young Men's Christian Association, a few academics (the president of Berea College and a professor from the University of Michigan), and the "famous gospel singer and hymn writer" Ira Sankey.

The book opens with a preface for parents and other adults that justifies the need for limited instruction of the young girl in certain delicate matters. Like all early sex educators, Wood-Allen acted on the belief that knowledge of sex is dangerous to young people unless it is meted out in small quantities. Her preface reassures parents that her approach will be cautious: "It is thought wise to put the information suited to different ages in different volumes so that the girl will find what meets her present need and not be led into fields of investigation wider than the immediate case demands."

The dramatis personae of *Young Girl* are Nina and her mother, Mrs. Grant, who, like the characters in Stall's book, are having a series of talks after the birth of a baby brother. The instruction begins with the usual descriptions of plant reproduction, pollen and the role of bees, and fish fertilization (favored, perhaps, by Victorian sex educators because it requires no embarrassing description of physical contact between the participants). Mrs. Grant proceeds to mammals' care of their offspring, and gingerly describes human birth. Sexual intercourse is only hinted at in delicate terms: "The germ of life . . . would never wake up unless it were touched by the power that only the father could give." Nina is warned that a good girl will not listen to her playmates' versions of these facts and is forearmed with a sample rebuff: " 'I would rather you would not tell me about it. I will ask my mother and she will tell me. Mother tells me everything that I ought to know and she tells it to me in such a way that makes it very sweet to me, and so I have my little secrets with mother, and not with other girls.' "

A chapter on moral heredity reveals Wood-Allen's predictable Lamarckian ideas. Mrs. Grant explains that her early lack of effort to control her bad temper has resulted in Nina's difficulties with the same trait. On the other hand, languages are easy for Nina to learn because her mother studied them diligently as a child. The point, of course, is that Nina must be made aware of the far-reaching consequences of her own behavior, which, presumably, she will pass on to her own children.

The next chapter is on masturbation. Girls are warned against this practice, but gently, as was appropriate for their presumed lesser temptation. As in the manuals for boys, constipation is discussed at length in connection with masturbation. (Sex educators reasoned that constipation produced pinworms, which led to local itching, which led to local scratching, handling of the genitals, and solitary vice.) The lack of fresh fruits and vegetables and whole grains in the American diet probably made constipation a universal condition, and dietary advice to relieve the problem became obligatory in sex education books. Tea and coffee were routinely forbidden, as were alcohol and tobacco (for men, that is; there was no question of a woman smoking). In *Young Girl*, Wood-Allen recommends "milk, eggs, oatmeal, entire wheat flour, and fruits."

After physical hygiene the doctor turns to mental hygiene: "Evil thoughts create actual poisons in the blood, good thoughts create life-giving forces." Posture (or "carriage") affects the mental state, and so it is important to stand upright in correct alignment. The value of work is extolled (surprisingly, she has "no objection to a girl learning to use nails, saw and hammer"), and the complementary value of wholesome play, such as gymnastics. Wood-Allen illustrates the evils of wrong recreation through an anecdote about a young man who died of delirium tremens after two weeks of "visiting saloons."

Wood-Allen emphasizes that girls should choose good reading (defined as "the books that make you desire to be better") from the categories of history and biography, science and art, travel and exploration, morals and religion. On no account are girls to read "silly stories" of robbers and pirates and bandits in scenes of murder and robbery and intrigue. Education is of value to a woman because it can be morally uplifting and is useful in running a household. Also it ensures that her children will not be ashamed of their mother. Anticipating that girl readers will begin to feel the burden of society's expectations a bit heavy on their sex at this point, Wood-Allen digresses here to explain that boys should be as pure and good as girls.

*Young Girl* mentions menstruation only obliquely: "some physical changes which take place at puberty of which I will more fully tell you as the time approaches." Without specifying why, Wood-Allen recommends plenty of sleep and exercise at puberty. Exercise is to be had most conveniently in the form of housework: "Dishwashing is especially beneficial as the hot water calls the blood to the hands and so helps to relieve the headache or backache" and "it is far better for the young girl at puberty to be gently active in household duties than to be lying around reading love stories."

In the concluding section Wood-Allen sums up *What a Young Girl Ought to Know*: women's work is to make a home for men and to train future men and women. Perhaps feeling the need to modify the harsh truth of this arrangement, she adds that this allows women the leisure to entertain: "If the mother, as well as the father, went away in the morning to business, and both came home tired at night, there would be little of the social life which we all find so enjoyable." She also notes encouragingly that women can use their free time to advance social causes such as temperance and social purity. (Like most Victorian writers, Wood-Allen assumed that her readership was of the privileged upper classes.) Thus, with this amount of information and advice, the young girl was considered appropriately equipped to face the storms of puberty.

## "Your Body Is Your Dwelling"

Wood-Allen's next book, *What a Young Woman Ought to Know* (1898), is intended for girls in their mid- to late teens, and is equally reticent in tone. However, this time the eminent persons cited on the opening pages are strong women who, in some way, had transcended the role limitations imposed on their sex and who were leaders in the feminist movement: May Wright Sewall, president of the International Council of Women and nominee of the International Congress of Women; Mary Lowe Dickinson, president of the National Council of Women and professor of literature at Denver University;

Matilda B. Carse, founder of the Woman's Temple, Chicago; Helen Campbell, dean of home economics at Kansas State University and author of *Prisoners of Poverty* and *Wage Earners;* Elisabeth Robinson Scovil, associate editor of the *Ladies' Home Journal;* and Elizabeth Cady Stanton, "noted woman suffragist." The roster is impressive, but if Wood-Allen selected these women because she admired their achievements, she did not permit their ideas to infiltrate her book for young women, nor did she allow her own success as a doctor and author to alter her stance on the importance of a woman's place in the home.

Sparing older readers another recitation of the birds and the bees, Wood-Allen launches immediately into practical matters, with a minimum of rhetoric and theology. The emphasis in *What a Young Woman Ought to Know* is on health: "Your body is your dwelling." After a discussion of diet and the need for plenty of sleep, she takes up a topic troublesome to the corseted Victorian woman—breathing. For many women of this era, when the eighteen-inch waist was the ideal of beauty, a deep breath was impossible. Wood-Allen considered the topic important enough to devote three chapters to it. After explaining the function of oxygen in the blood and the action of the diaphragm, she describes the damage done by tight lacing. Not only is breathing hindered, but the stomach and the liver are squeezed up under the diaphragm or down into the pelvis, with consequent malfunctions. The circulation is hampered and the heart overloaded. Sometimes a condition called "corset liver" results, in which the organ is pinched into two parts connected only by a thin strip of tissue. Wood-Allen pronounces judgment on these fashionable tortures by declaring that a tiny waist is a deformity and a mutilation.*

Exercise, therefore, should always be taken in loose clothing. Wood-Allen's first recommendation, of course, is the "home gymnasium," that is, housework. But skating, lawn tennis, and swimming are also approved, as is bicycle riding (*if* the girl does not sit on her perineum). Dancing is excellent exercise in itself, but cannot be recommended because it involves late hours, immodest dress, and heavy late suppers, and may lead to promiscuous associations.

After some words on bathing and care of the complexion, she moves on to a detailed explanation of the function and hygiene of menstruation. The female organs of reproduction are briefly described, although there is no diagram and no mention of the external

---

*Clothing reform was a constant plank in the feminist platform. The loose Turkish trousers and tunic designed by Amelia Bloomer were worn for a time by a few leading suffragist women as a protest.

genitalia. Then Wood-Allen pictures the internal events of the menses, betraying the fact that she, like her medical contemporaries, believed that ovulation and menstruation were simultaneous:

> The uterus is lined by a mucous membrane similar to that which lines the mouth, and at this time of ovulation this membrane becomes swollen and soft, and little hemorrhages, or bleedings occur for three or four days, the blood passing away through the vagina. This is called menstruation.

It is not necessary that a woman be a periodical semi-invalid, says the doctor; menstruation should be painless, but the majority of civilized women suffer more or less. She blames this on tight, unhealthful clothing, lack of exercise, constipation, twisted postures, standing on one foot, and disturbed nerves from reading novels (the latter because it causes an abnormal excitement of the sexual organs, and can also cause premature sexual physical development).

Precautions should be taken during the menstrual period, since the girl's energy is being used to "establish a new function." She should guard herself from cold, overexertion, social dissipation, and mental excitement, especially the aforesaid novel reading. An abdominal support bandage can be used for taking pressure off the bowels. Contrary to old wives' tales, it is all right to change underwear and to wash, although full tub baths are not advisable. Wet feet and clothes can be dangerous at this time because the girl is weaker and more susceptible to infection.

If she has severe pain, a girl should assume the "recumbent position," drink warm liquids, and apply warm cloths (but she should never make use of alcohol, either internally or externally). It is a bad practice to consult traveling doctors or take hot douches. Remedies for extremely heavy flow are bed rest, cold cloths over the abdomen and between the thighs, and two or three enemas a day. Wood-Allen cautions that nervous strain, such as the pressures of school, may stop the menses, but assures readers that this is not a symptom of tuberculosis. Rather, the reverse is true; tuberculosis can lead to cessation of menstruation.

Wood-Allen's description of Victorian sanitary arrangements for menstrual "protection" in *Young Woman* gives us some insight into the difficulties of the curse in the days before tampons:

> I would suggest that the napkins be fastened to straps that go over the shoulder and are then joined together in front and back to an end piece, on each of which a button is sewn. Buttonholes in the napkins at the corners, diagonal from each other, will make them easily attached or removed.

Directions for sewing napkins follow.

While she is on the subject of vaginal discharges, Wood-Allen takes up the matter of leukorrhea. This is not a disease, she maintains, but results from congestion of the blood vessels due to improper dress, taking cold, or "a debilitated condition of the stomach" (providing another example of the curious but common assumption of the times that the reproductive and digestive systems were somehow closely linked).

After such a long discourse on menstruation, Wood-Allen mercifully gets to the point on masturbation:

> It destroys mental power and memory, it blotches the complexion, dulls the eye, takes away the strength, and may cause insanity. It is a habit most difficult to overcome, and may not only last for years, but in its tendency be transmitted to one's children.

In an echo of the doctrine of seminal power, she states that the release of sexual energy through masturbation represents a "waste of vital force" and implies that the expenditure of this force is acceptable only in marital intercourse for the purpose of procreation: "One can feel justified to lose a part of her own life if she is conferring life upon others, but to indulge in such a waste of vital force merely for pleasure is certainly never excusable." Self-abuse may be accomplished by fantasies of love making, without manual stimulation. Reading romances can lead to this mental masturbation. To overcome the habit, girls should remember that sex is holy and intended for reproduction. They should avoid pelvic congestion from constipation or tight clothes, and keep the mind healthfully occupied with other thoughts.

Next the doctor talks about flirting. Later sex educators were to call it "petting" and devote many fevered pages to exploring its evils. Wood-Allen's arguments foreshadow the writings of Ann Landers and Evelyn Duvall. Many girls feel, she says, that they have to allow intimacies to get young men to notice them. They may think a few stolen kisses and unobserved hand pressures don't matter, but they are "playing with the fire of physical passion." Moreover, young men talk about flirts. A girl who arouses a boy may cause him to lose his honor and purity by going to prostitutes; it is a girl's responsibility to discourage intimacies and keep matters within the bounds of propriety even during her engagement. As for friendships between girls, they, too, should be kept at a physical distance. The attitude of "gushy" girls who fondle and kiss "if probed thoroughly might be found to be a sort of perversion, a sex mania." As a matter of fact, young girls should keep everybody at a physical distance, and only kiss their mothers. This doctrine of distance is reinforced in the next chapter on venereal disease. Millions die annually from these diseases, which can be transmitted by a kiss. For further facts, girls are referred to *What a Young Man Ought to Know*.

Wood-Allen's interest in eugenics is reflected in several chapters on heredity, which caution girls to choose a husband carefully on the basis of his behavior and genetic inheritance. The concluding chapters deal with the engagement and the wedding, bringing the reader to the next book in the series.

Predictably, Emma Drake's two books match the advice Sylvanus Stall had provided in his companion volumes for men. *What a Young Wife Ought to Know* (1901) glorifies home and family, and *What a Woman of Forty-five Ought to Know* (1902) is a less than comforting guide through menopause. Like the other volumes of the Self and Sex series, these books for women were very popular and ran to several editions—*Young Woman* was being reprinted as late as 1936.

## Earlier Titles for Girls and Young Women

In Chapter 1 we saw how Lyman Beecher Sperry's *Confidential Talks with Young Men* and Wood-Allen's *Almost a Man* preceded the publication of the Self and Sex volumes for boys and young men. In the same way, ground had been broken for the sex instruction of girls and young women by Sperry's *Confidential Talks with Young Women* and Wood-Allen's own *Almost a Woman*. Both predated the more popular Self and Sex books, and both set themes that sex educators were to reiterate and elaborate for many years to come.

Published in 1893, Sperry's *Confidential Talks with Young Women* was the very first sex advice manual addressed to teenage girls. It established many of the themes that were later orchestrated by Wood-Allen and her followers, including the benefits of fresh air, moderate exercise, and healthful diet; the dangers of late parties, masturbation, sentimental novels, indiscriminate kissing, and wet feet and fatigue during menstruation. We can be sure that Wood-Allen was influenced by, or at least was aware of, *Confidential Talks with Young Women* because she wrote the introduction (Wood-Allen had already gained some recognition with the publication of her first Teaching Truth booklet the previous year).

Although Sperry was as obsessed as his contemporaries with preserving virginity and preventing masturbation, his primary concern
in *Confidential Talks with Young Women* is the unhealthful practices and social expectations that made early invalids of many wom-
en—the lack of fresh air and exercise and the stifling, choking
burden of fashionable dress: "The expected physical condition of
the modern American woman over thirty years of age is a sofa, a
shawl, and the neuralgia." Modern society (of 1893) puts obstacles to
healthful development in women's way, says Sperry: malnutrition,
the practice of keeping girls indoors—and worst of all, fashionable
dress. Corseting and tight lacing can be blamed for prolapsed or
tipped uteruses, and, characteristically, Sperry provides a careful anatomical description of how this can happen. Crowding and injury
of the rectum and the bladder can also take place in corset-squeezed
abdomens. The development of the sexual organs can be affected
and, consequently, all maturing. Western man is horrified at the Chinese practice of foot binding, yet corseting and lacing are every bit as
cruelly wrong. Tight shoes and garters and the weight of heavy skirts
also hamper circulation and development. Sperry quotes from *The
Relation of Dress to Vice* by Frances E. Willard as he maintains that
hampering dress is a remnant of primitive society: "Every punctured
ear, bandaged waist, and high heeled shoe is a reminder that manhood and womanhood are yet under the curse transmitted by their
ignorant and semi-barbarous ancestry."

What, then, could the young girl who wanted to be healthy
change about her clothes to make them comfortable but still not be
an object of ridicule on the street? Like many "radical" thinkers of
the day, Sperry admired Amelia Bloomer's costume in principle but
did not seriously advocate wearing it in broad daylight. He proposed
instead a three-point program of moderate dress reform. To para-
phrase:

1. Leave off corsets and loosen the dress.
2. Reduce the weight of clothing and shorten skirts so they do not drag
   on the floor.
3. Clothe each limb, legs as well as arms, individually and evenly (presumably, he means *under* the skirts).

Many women are reluctant to adopt dress reform because they
fear men may be hostile to it. Nonsense, says Sperry: "If the women
will but make convenient, comfortable, healthful, modest dress *fashionable,* the men will admire it and praise it far more than they ever
approved the grotesque upholstery, drapery, flummery and murder-

ous toggery in which women have so long and so submissively masqueraded." As support, Sperry quotes at length a corset manufacturer who has found it profitable to switch over to producing loose "waists" with buttons for attaching skirts. The standard corset measurements, he explains, are bust fourteen inches larger than the waist and hips sixteen inches larger (36–22–38, for instance). His new product, the "waists," have a difference of only ten inches between waist and hip. True, they do have steel reinforcement up the front and sides, but this can easily be slipped out if the wearer wishes to be completely unfettered. The manufacturer describes this new healthful Victorian version of le minimum: "At the foundation is the union undergarment, covering the arms, legs and body in one piece. Then there will be the stockings and the waist, the stockings being supported by hose supporters attached to the waist. Over this cotton drawers can be fashioned directly to the waist; or, the cotton drawers and waist-cover can be combined in one garment, to be used in place of the old fashioned chemise. Over this again is a single skirt; better still, the divided skirt. This with a dress in which the waist and skirt are made in one piece, completes the costume."

Sperry's depiction of the physical and mental changes of puberty may seem exaggerated to a modern reader, but it was probably based on the doctor's clinical observation of the Victorian teenage girl, who was expected to be occasionally neurasthenic and hysterical and who referred to her menstrual period as being "unwell." The mental manifestations of puberty, Sperry says, are a new weariness and indifference to passing events, bashfulness, a fondness for love stories, giggling and gossiping with one close friend, a tendency to be absent-minded, nervous, and notional. A girl may often "feel like having a good cry about it." Although the physical changes of puberty result in a glow of attractiveness, the subjective symptoms are not so pleasant, he adds: "Quite likely you experienced wandering pains and shifting aches, heaviness in the small of the back, a sort of pressure in the spine, and a great many little 'bad feelings.' " These and other discomforts of painful menstruation are the habit of civilized, sedentary women, explains Sperry, and are not at all the normal state in nature.

Sperry is quite comfortable in describing the anatomy of menstruation, including the function of the ovum and the sperm, although he, like Wood-Allen, is convinced that ovulation occurs during the menses. He is not so comfortable, though, in advising girls on the hygiene of their periods, and suggests that a girl ask her mother or a trusted teacher about this or go to a woman doctor: "Fortunately, there are now many educated and trustworthy physicians of your own sex to whom you may properly and safely apply for counsel in such matters. You may thereby avoid the strain which, very naturally (although unnecessarily) you might experience in calling upon a physician of the opposite sex."

Now Sperry turns to a subject he finds even less congenial: masturbation. He turns over the chapter to Mrs. E. P. Miller, author of "A Mother's Advice," explaining that "it seems most fitting that the needed words of admonition should come direct from one who is a mother as well as a physician." Mrs. Miller takes over with gusto: "When I see a little girl or a young lady wasted and weak and listless, with great hollow eyes and a sort of sallow tint on the haggard face, with the red hue of the lips faded, the ears white like marble and the face covered with pimples, I dread lest they have committed the sin which, if not abandoned, will lead them down to death." Many women "die of consumption and liver disease and brain disease and many other diseases just because they have wasted their best blood and weakened the system by this vile habit. Some become idiots . . . some become crazy; in the insane asylums all over the land are very many who have practiced self-abuse. Many of those who commit suicide do it because they practiced this habit when they were young."

*Confidential Talks with Young Women* concludes with a promising picture of the future of feminism, which is, unfortunately, short on specifics: "Woman may, if she will, secure perfect development of all her powers, perfect freedom of action in all spheres of activity possible for her, and perfect equality with man, socially, politically and commercially."

Mary Wood-Allen's *Almost a Woman* was published in 1897 as a companion volume to *Almost a Man* (1895), and although it appeared in the same year as *What a Young Girl Ought to Know*, it almost certainly is an earlier work. It clearly shows the author's lack of commitment to female emancipation, and, like the moralistic tale of Guy, and Frank, and Carl, and Rob, uses fiction to make its point.

The prelude finds Mr. and Mrs. Wayne discussing their thirteen-year-old daughter, Helen. "Have you explained her approaching womanhood to her?" asks Mr. Wayne. His wife responds that she has been waiting for the right moment: "I have thought that perhaps she would indicate by some question that her mind was becoming ready for the disclosure. It always seems to me that to force information before the mind is ready to receive it, is to jeopardize its reception."

"Don't wait, Mary" says her husband sternly. They agree to seize the first opportunity.

In the next chapter that opportunity presents itself. Helen and her father are alone in the house, and he uses the occasion for a chat on the dangers of being free with young men. Helen is troubled by the double standard: "But, Father, tell me why it's so much more important for girls to be particular about what they do than for boys?"

"Well, it's not," he says, but adds that everybody thinks it is. He explains the high ideals society holds up for women, and reads her several pieces of literature to illustrate, among them this passage from John Ruskin's *Sesame and Lillies:*

> Woman's power is for rule, not for battle, and her intellect is not for invention or creation, but for sweet ordering, arrangement and decision. Her great function is Praise. There is not a war in the world, no, nor an injustice, but you women are answerable for it, not in that you have provoked, but in that you have not hindered. Men, by their nature, are prone to fight. They will fight for any cause or none. It is for you to choose their cause for them, and to forbid when there is no cause. There is no suffering, no injustice, no misery in the earth, but the guilt of it lies with you.

Helen is polite but not impressed. She chafes at the limitations imposed on her by her sex. Her father's answers are unconvincing, and our sympathy is all with Helen. "It seems so much grander to be a man than a woman. A man's life is so much freer, and he can do so much greater things, you know. Of course, I shall try to be a good woman, but I wish women could do big things, the way men can . . . women just sit in the house and look on. I'd like to *do* something."

"It only seems like men do bigger things," her father responds, "it is *mind* that does the real work and women have minds, you know."

"Yes, I know, but they must devote their minds to cooking and dishwashing," she says. But Mr. Wayne persists, and eventually convinces her to be content with her lot, because after all, while "man makes *things;* woman makes *men.*"

Mrs. Wayne soon has her turn. As she and Helen are sitting by the front window, a flirtatious young woman of Helen's acquaintance passes by. This leads to talk about the impropriety of accepting expensive presents from young men and allowing them to take liberties.

"Mother," says Helen after a pause, as two girls pass the house with their arms about each other's waists, "Don't you think it silly for girls to be so 'spooney?' Lucy is always having such lover-like friends and then quarreling with them. Now, she and Nellie are go-

ing to have a mock wedding next week. They call themselves husband and wife even now—isn't that silly?" Mrs. Wayne thinks it is
worse than silly—"morbid unnatural sentimentality" she calls it.

(The subject of quasi-sexual relationships between girls occurs
frequently in these books, demonstrating the Victorian abhorrence to
any hint of homosexuality. Although affectionate friendships between young women have never been uncommon, the hugging and
kissing of Victorian girlfriends was probably a response to the absence of physical affection in the home. Forbidden any other expression, the sexuality of young women emerged in such fevered
and sentimental attractions. While a few of these romances may have
been lesbian love affairs, the great majority of them were probably
nongenital.)

The next time Mrs. Wayne is alone with Helen she delicately
brings up the subject of how girls become women. It soon becomes
clear that while Helen has absorbed a detailed knowledge of human
physiology at school, the reproductive system has never been mentioned in those lessons. The words "womb," "uterus," and "vagina"
are new to her, and she is surprised to hear about "the little room
where the baby grows." She shows an apprehensive interest in her
mother's explanation of menstruation, but is on more familiar
ground when the talk shifts to the internal damage done by the corset. (Mrs. Wayne shows her a drawing comparing the ideal shape of
the Venus de Milo with the corseted figure of a popular actress.)
Helen asks for an explanation of the plight of a girlfriend who has
had an illegitimate child, which gives her mother a chance to ex-
pound on the evils of permitting "even the slightest unwarranted
familiarity." With married people, on the other hand, "it is perfectly
proper for them to do what before would not have been proper."
That proper action needs some clarification, so Mrs. Wayne explains, but not very directly: "You can understand that, for the
spermatozoa to be placed where they can find their way into the
uterus, means a very close and familiar relationship of the man and
woman."

No Wood-Allen book would be complete without some mention
of the obligation to improve heredity by right action, and the related
importance of temperance. Alcohol and tobacco are evil, and she
illustrates that fact with two stories: the first about a little boy who
attempted to murder his baby brother with scissors because his father was an alcoholic and had passed on the mental degeneration to
him, and the second about a tobacco-addicted baby born to a woman
who was an inveterate smoker and who found that the only way to
quiet her child's cries was to put the pipe between its lips.

At the end of this model of parental instruction the reader finds Helen resigned to her fate. She says, a bit sadly, "I think after this I'll try to feel that even I am of importance to the world, instead of regretting that I am not a man."

Sperry's and Wood-Allen's books are typical of the flavor and content of most sex education books for girls from the turn of the century through its first and second decades. The late Victorian social hygienists were prolific, and many other titles exist, among them *The Doctor's Plain Talk to Young Women* (1902) by Virgil Primrose English, *Personal Information for Girls* (1909) by Ernest Edwards, and *Confidences* (1910) by Edith Belle Lowry. While sex educators continued to caution girls against coquettish behavior and too much exercise, however, the literature for boys began to urge them to strive toward a redefined—and impossibly rigorous—masculine ideal.

## BIBLIOGRAPHY

Drake, Emma Frances. *What a Woman of Forty-five Ought to Know.* Self and Sex Series. Philadelphia: Vir Publishing Co., 1902.

———. *What a Young Wife Ought to Know.* Self and Sex Series. Philadelphia: Vir Publishing Co., 1901; rev. ed., 1908.

Edwards, Ernest. *Personal Information for Girls.* New York: R. F. Fenno, 1909.

English, Virgil Primrose. *The Doctor's Plain Talk to Young Women.* Cleveland: Ohio State Publishing Co., 1902.

Howe, Joseph William. *Excessive Venery, Masturbation, and Continence.* New York: E. B. Treat, 1887; reprint, New York: Arno Press, 1974.

Ingraham, Charles A. *Steps up Life's Ladder: An Old Doctor's Letters to a Young Friend.* Poughkeepsie, NY: A. V. Haught Co., 1905.

Lowry, Edith Belle. *Confidences: Talks with a Young Girl Concerning Herself.* Chicago: Forbes and Co., 1910.

Parkhurst, Charles H. *Talks to Young Women.* New York: Century, 1895; rev. ed., 1897.

Sperry, Lyman Beecher. *Confidential Talks with Young Women.* Chicago: Fleming H. Revell Co., 1893.

Wood-Allen, Mary. *Adolescence.* American Motherhood Leaflets no. 32. Cooperstown, NY: Crist, Scott and Parshall, 1907.

———. *Almost a Man.* Ann Arbor, MI: Wood-Allen Publishing Co., 1895, 1897.

———. *Almost a Man.* Teaching Truth Series. Cooperstown, NY: Crist, Scott and Parshall, 1907.

———. *Almost a Woman.* Ann Arbor, MI: Wood-Allen Publishing Co., 1897.

———. *Almost a Woman.* Teaching Truth Series. Cooperstown, NY: Crist, Scott and Parshall, 1907.

————. *Caring for the Baby*. Teaching Truth Series. Cooperstown, NY: Crist, Scott and Parshall, 1907.

————. *Child-Confidence Rewarded*. Teaching Truth Series. Ann Arbor, MI: Wood-Allen Publishing Co., 1903; Cooperstown, NY: Crist, Scott and Parshall, 1903.

————. *Ideal Married Life: A Book for All Husbands and Wives*. New York: Fleming H. Revell Co., 1901.

————. *Keep Mother and Me Intimate*. American Motherhood Leaflets no. 31. Cooperstown, NY: Crist, Scott and Parshall, 1907.

————. *Making the Best of Our Children*, ed. by Rose Woodallen Chapman. Chicago: A. C. McClurg and Co., 1909

————. *The Marvels of Our Bodily Dwelling; Physiology Made Interesting; Suitable as a Text-book or Reference Book in Schools, or for Pleasant Home Reading*. Ann Arbor, MI: Wood-Allen Publishing Co., 1895, 1896; Philadelphia: Vir Publishing Co., 1915.

————. *A Noble Father*. American Motherhood Leaflets no. 10. Cooperstown, NY: Crist, Scott and Parshall, 1907.

————. *Teaching Truth*. Ann Arbor, MI: Wood-Allen Publishing Co., 1892.

————. *Teaching Truth*. Teaching Truth Series. Ann Arbor, MI: Wood-Allen Publishing Co., 1903; Cooperstown, NY: Crist, Scott and Parshall, 1907.

————. *What a Young Girl Ought to Know*. Self and Sex Series. Philadelphia: Vir Publishing Co., 1897; rev. ed., 1905.

————. *What a Young Woman Ought to Know*. Self and Sex Series. Philadelphia: Vir Publishing Co., 1898; rev. eds., 1905, 1913.

# 3

# *The Bully Boys and the Rosy Girls*

Theodore Roosevelt, like Queen Victoria, was one of those leaders who came to represent the ideals and aspirations of an age, who symbolized the unfocused yearnings of their people. A complex and fascinating character with enormous charm but many inner contradictions, Roosevelt was perceived by the popular imagination as the champion of American capitalism, and a man who had used his fierce competitive instincts to create his own manhood. Roosevelt was wracked with asthma as a child; his illness kept him at home and isolated him from his peers. Although he disciplined his mind, he grew up with a feeble body. As a young teenager, he was so shamed at being easily overpowered by a group of young toughs that he determined to build himself a strong body. Using great resources of willpower and energy, he did just that, and became a man whose skill and endurance in the outdoor life won him the loyalty and companionship of seasoned cowboys, grizzled soldiers in the Spanish-American War, and big-game hunters in Africa.

This aspect of Roosevelt's colorful life became an example for young boys in America: the idea that virile manhood must be created by strenuous self-discipline, vigorous effort, and self-denial. Along with this muscular ideal went a denial of the feminine quality: although women were to be treated with almost reverent respect, the ultimate insult to a man was to be called a "sissy"—a word derived from "sister." Men were not allowed to express their more sensitive, aesthetic, and emotional nature for fear of discrediting their hard-won masculinity. American men are straitjacketed by this syndrome even today, and have only recently begun to struggle against it.

The sex educators seized on this pervasive and popular ideal of manhood. They encouraged the enthusiasm for body-building, outdoor sports, and self-discipline as a method of diverting sexual energies and squelching masturbatory temptations. In a book of instruction to parents, Sex Education, author Ira Solomon Wile said in 1912: "Activity diverts energy into channels free from sexual suggestion. Idleness and laziness involve a sluggish circulation and a will flabby from disuse. There is little manliness to withstand the assaults of the degenerate sex lore of the gang, the train of horrors like dance-halls, saloons, and boat excursions."

Like the Victorians, sex educators in the early years of this century were primarily interested in sex education as a form of sex prevention. Their methods differed from those of their predecessors in that, instead of terrifying their young readers, they emphasized the joys of building manliness through exercise and self-discipline. In 1914, William Trufant Foster edited a collection of essays entitled The Social Emergency that distilled the ideas of the time on the aims of sex education. The essays had been adapted from a series of lectures delivered at Reed College by authorities in the field to an audience of teachers and social workers. They reveal an almost unanimous agreement on the proper content of education in sex. (The "emergency" in the title refers not to an epidemic of venereal disease, as might be suspected, but to the breaking of silence on the subject of sex and the lack of competent teachers.) Although the contributors to this book were still firmly convinced that conservation of semen was essential to manhood, they were beginning to rebel against the earlier hysterical fear of self-abuse. "To warn boys against horrible effects of masturbation and to tell them things not to do is a poor method. It is far better to explain that by keeping clean a boy may acquire virility," wrote Harry Hascall Moore, whose invocation of the usefulness of sports in helping boys to keep pure here became the theme of his own book, Keeping in Condition, published in 1916:

> Athletics are to be recommended as possessing a positive prophylactic value against the indulgence of sensual propensities. Physical exercise serves as an outlet for the superabundant energy which might otherwise be directed toward the sexual sphere. . . .

The Teddy Roosevelt ideal emerges clearly in this passage by another contributor to Foster's book, Edward O. Sisson:

> The lad who plays vigorously, even violently; who can "get his second wind," turn a handspring, do a good cross-country run, swim the river, possesses a great bulwark of defense against sexual vice, especially in its secret forms.

Andrew C. Smith's essay summarizes the content of sex education for a boy, which, according to Smith, should begin "when more thrilling sensations command his attention." The boy should be taught that this new function is for reproduction only, that sexual activity is not necessary for health, and that involuntary emissions are normal and not harmful. Moore, in his own essay, adds that boys should also be disabused of belief in the double standard and the idea that gonorrhea is no worse than a bad cold. A girl, however, needs only to be instructed on menstruation and to be impressed with the idea that the purpose of her sex mechanism is maternity. She should be taught to guard her purity against both sexes, and "it will only fortify her maidenliness to tell her that much of the world is deceitful and degrading in sex matters."

One of the first books for young men to advocate the muscular path to sexual abstinence was *Helps to Health and Purity* by Elisha Alonzo King, a tiny pocket-sized handbook that appeared in 1903 (although it had been published in 1897 under the title *A Talk to Men*). King also later wrote *Clean and Strong* (1909, 1917), a book with similar content, for the United Society of Christian Endeavor. After providing reassurances about the normalcy of nocturnal emissions, King discourses on the evils of masturbation. He recommends cold baths as a remedy to temptation and advises at length on techniques for overcoming constipation. The second half of the book describes health-building exercises, each one beginning with the command "Attention!" A photograph of King's exercise class—rows of leotard-clad figures with folded arms—adorns this section.

The organization that most clearly grew out of this American ideal of manhood is the Boy Scouts, which was founded in 1910. It is no accident that Teddy Roosevelt is listed in the first handbook as honorary vice-president, right after the obligatory first choice of then-President William Taft. An advertisement for shredded wheat on the inside cover of that first handbook gives the flavor of the 1911 Boy Scout philosophy: "Building buster boys is bully business!" That basic philosophy has not changed much in sixty-eight years—Scouting is still characterized by an enthusiasm for strenuous outdoor exercise and clean living. Taking cold baths and avoiding constipation remained a ubiquitous refrain in Boy Scout literature and scoutmasters' lectures for the majority of those years.

The sexual attitudes reflected in the 1911 Boy Scout *Official Handbook for Boys* were equally predictable and long-lived. Chapter 5, titled "Health and Endurance," was written by George J. Fisher, a doctor with the physical department of the Young Men's Christian Association. The last paragraph, headed "Conservation," explains in careful euphemisms the need to avoid wrong habits and retain the sex fluid for manliness. Readers are referred to Winfield Scott Hall's *From Youth into Manhood* (1909) for further information. Thirty-four years later, in the 1945 edition of the handbook, the passage remained substantially unchanged, although a few words about nocturnal emissions had been added and Fisher had become national Scout commissioner. Only after a protest in that year by sexologist Alfred Kinsey was the sexual advice modernized. (The 1972 and 1978 editions of the handbook only advise boys who have questions about sexual matters to talk them over with parents and spiritual or medical advisers.)

## The Bully Boys

The most full-blown example of the "bully boys" school of thought is Harry Hascall Moore's *Keeping in Condition; Handbook on Training for Older Boys* (1916). The book's contents and its bluff and hearty tone are so representative of its type that it is worth examining in some detail. In the preface the author makes it clear that he is making "an attempt to set up an ideal of vigorous manhood, a program of training now used by many expert leaders of boys to relieve them of the sex excitation and temptations so clearly part of the dangers to our present-day social life." He proposes to lay out "all the essentials of training for manhood—exercise, fresh air, diet, rest, and 'the control of inner force.' " The book is illustrated with photographs of groups of boys engaged in various manly outdoor activities: climbing a snow-covered mountain peak, finishing a race, diving into a lake, shooting rapids in a canoe, and "roasting 'hot-dogs' over fires built in the rain after a morning hike." The frontispiece adds a reference to Spartan life with a photograph of a Greek statue, "The relay runner."

Moore begins with a pep talk about the six qualities of virility—strong muscles, endurance, energy, courage, self-control, and will-power. Young readers are exhorted to get right to work on building their manhood now before it is too late: "It is the function of the boy to develop the powers that will be used in adult activities, such as vital and nervous energy, skill, will power, and courage. This development cannot be secured after maturity." Self-development aimed toward the attainment of the racial and national ideal is a boy's responsibility.

So to work. A boy should start the year by visiting the doctor and getting a clean bill of health, and by taking two or three photographs of the body in various positions. This is for comparison as body building progresses, so that the boy can have a plan of competing with himself. The best exercises are baseball, rowing, canoeing, skating, and especially hiking. Boxing, wrestling, and gymnastics are good, too, if they can be done in the open air. A set of calisthenics is also given for posture and muscle building. Exercise should be followed by a short warm bath, a cold plunge, and a rubdown.

The diet Moore recommends seems to our sensibilities to be deficient in bulk—no salads, fresh vegetables, or raw fruit—and very heavy in starch and fats. "Bread and milk," he says, "provide all the important elements in food." Each mouthful of this diet is to be chewed thoroughly to a paste, and coffee, tea, alcohol, and tobacco are absolutely forbidden. Fresh air is an important element in training for manhood; the candidate should exercise in it at least two hours a day and sleep out-of-doors if at all possible.

This hard-won virility can be lost by yielding to the temptation of self-abuse. A boy who would be a real man must be mentally clean and keep dangerous thoughts and suggestions away by willpower or with physical exertion: "By *immediately* turning to vigorous exercise, or hard mental or physical work, this impulse may be converted in a wonderful yet mysterious manner into a great constructive force in his life." In summary, "He who would possess virility must work for it."

Virility can also be endangered by tuberculosis, colds, typhoid fever, venereal disease, constipation, and worry about nocturnal emissions. This last should be no cause for alarm, says Moore. The manly essence of the fluids is not lost in natural emissions; only when a boy allows himself to become sexually excited does the discharge involve the whole system. Therefore, manhood candidates should keep away from suggestive pictures and stories, "certain vaudeville acts," and all impure thinking. Moore illustrates with an anecdote: "A short time ago a football player on one of the big university teams began to play poorly. His coach investigated the trouble and found that the man had a suggestive picture hanging in his bedroom. The coach at once tore it down . . ." and the player's game improved very soon afterward.

Moore briefly touches on the mechanics of plant and animal reproduction, ending with the union of the sperm and the ovum.

When it comes to human beings, however, he says only: "In a true man, the beauty and wonder of it all awakens tenderness and a protective sense toward all women and girls." Moore returns to the issue of feminine delicacy repeatedly in *Keeping in Condition:* "A youth should regard all girls as the future mothers of the race" and "should treat every girl as he expects other fellows to treat his own sister." Girls are to be given special consideration during those times when they are sensitive to exercise because of their "monthly sickness."

For these and other reasons, the sex drive, which can be compared to fire or rushing water, must be controlled for good use. Indeed, "it is not enough to repress the sex instinct; it must be directed into constructive activities." There is a temptation to gratify desire, "the race instinct," with prostitutes or immoral girls. This must be resisted by keeping in mind the dangers of venereal disease. Remember, sex is not necessary for health. Controlling his instincts is "the biggest fight ever waged by man—a fight in secret—without applause."

Introducing another major theme, the implications of manhood training for race progress, Moore explains that it is important to consider heredity when choosing a mate. He adds, however, that it is not true that acquired characteristics are transmitted to one's children. National progress also calls for virile men. There are certain political and social problems on which a real man must take a firm stand: child labor, trade unionism, unemployment, and alcohol abuse. The nation needs virile men in the professions and the sciences, in business and trade, labor, public office, and social reform. In short, national purity equals national power.

Many similar books for boys were published during the two decades before World War I. The title recommended in the Boy Scout handbook of 1911—Hall's *From Youth into Manhood*—was published by the Young Men's Christian Association, which took up the promotion of muscular manhood with zeal. A prolific pamphleteer for sex education, Hall was a professor of physiology at Northwestern University Medical School. His pamphlets were not limited to a male audience and included *Margaret, the Doctor's Daughter,* published by the American Medical Association in 1911. Hall wrote a second book for boys in 1913 with the triple title *Father and Son; John's Vacation; What John Saw in the Country.* Since the vacation was at a farm with the usual component of copulating livestock, what John saw was sufficiently surprising to prompt him to ask his father a number of interesting questions. In response, however,

John's father limits himself to the standard advice about seminal conservation and good health habits.

Another prolific producer of pamphlets was Edward Bok, whose Books of Self-Knowledge for Young People and Parents grew out of articles on sexual subjects previously published in the *Ladies' Home Journal*. These small thin volumes of advice on intimate matters sold for twenty-five cents, and had various authors. Volume 2 of the series is typical—*When a Boy Becomes a Man* (1912) by H. Bisseker, an English schoolmaster, who addresses boys from ages thirteen to fifteen on the dual themes of the perils of masturbation and the benefits of health.

## Contesting Biology

Despite the emphasis that the virility advocates placed on the positive rewards of physical development in these books, the theory itself is in many ways grounded in disgust of the human body and represents an effort to control, and thereby overcome, the fact of man's animal nature. Thus it is not surprising that alongside the health and conditioning books there appeared a number of works that border on misanthropy in the stern relish with which they hold forth on the horrors of the body and of sexuality in particular. This attitude is most clearly evident in books written for girls (which emphasized the weaknesses of the female body), although it is not limited to them. A good example is *Confidential Chats with Girls* (1911) by William Lee Howard, which makes the "bully boys" books seem benevolent by contrast.

Reflecting the social changes of the Industrial Revolution that were beginning to result in the employment of large numbers of women in the factories, Howard addresses himself, with considerable condescension, to working girls. He defines his ground right from the beginning: "I do not intend to talk to you about the process of procreation or the physiology of conception." That can be read in other books. Rather, he intends to convey the warning that a girl who does not "protect her growth may ruin herself that, when she marries, she is unable to be a mother." A worthy message, although it "may seem a little indelicate," he cautions.

Launching into instruction on the care of the female sex organs, Howard explains that the ovaries are sensitive to emotion and movement. (The belief that the developing female sexual organs required a girl to be extraordinarily careful of her body appeared regularly in early sex education books. It was felt that jumping, running, and standing would tangle and twist the uterus and ovaries, or even jar them loose from their moorings entirely.) At puberty a girl should cease all rough play, sports, late dancing, and standing for long periods, says Howard. For the first two years after the onset of menstruation she should have no exercise except walking, swimming, and "bending of the body." Sledding is especially dangerous in that it may cause a rupture or strain of the ovaries or womb. Girls who disregard this advice may later regret it: "The ovaries may be so twisted and put out of order that nothing can be done for them in later life but to cut them out with a knife." Exercise during a menstrual period may displace the womb and cause difficulties in pregnancy: "the child is smothered while trying to grow, and then must come a horrible operation."

A girl should stay at home and rest during her period, Howard declares. To emphasize the point, he tells a tale about a young girl with menstrual pain who asked to go home from school. Her unfeeling teacher sent her to the principal, who asked embarrassing questions. A few days later, when the girl returned to school, the boys laughed at her. According to Howard, her mortification was so great that she attempted (by some unexplained means) to stop her menstral flow, which resulted in permanent internal damage. Furthermore, school is also harmful because of the physical stress of gymnastics classes. Girls who are too shy to ask permission to go to the bathroom may develop menstrual irregularity from retention of urine.

Beware of mumps; they can destroy the ovaries, Howard warns. But the worst fate of all is reserved for the girl who goes to dances lightly clothed, in short sleeves and low neck. She will surely end up in the doctor's hands or become a drug fiend.

Next comes a peculiar passage in which Howard unwittingly reveals a deep revulsion for the feminine body. Girls have bad odors, he says, but saturating the system with many glasses of water dilutes them so that "scarcely any of them will make their presence known to those around you." The effect of this accusation on an adolescent girl's self-confidence must have been devastating.

In a section on health and hygiene, even pimples are made a source of guilt: "Muddy and contaminating thoughts will cause a muddy skin." In a set piece of advice that holds the rudiments of the standard pimple talk for teens, he admonishes: (1) don't squeeze; (2) use your own brush; (3) ignore ads for remedies; (4) avoid constipation; and (5) go to a reputable doctor. And don't kiss other girls, he adds.

Howard's dietary advice in *Confidential Chats with Girls* is also eccentric. Cereal and stewed fruit should be eaten for breakfast. The author agrees with "most girls" that eggs, fish, and milk are repulsive. In any case, one should never drink milk with meat. Eating before bed is perfectly all right, as are candy, pickles, and almost anything else one wants to eat—as long as the bowels are kept open.

Like most of his contemporaries, Howard puts great faith in the healthfulness of cold baths. He also advises girls to perform "waist exercises" regularly, and to take sodium phosphate once a week (as a laxative). He vehemently attacks the rats and falls with which young women elaborate their coiffures because, he says, "dead" hair smells and such hairstyles may lead to baldness. Another Edwardian favorite, the high collar, also reaps his scorn: tight collars with points up under the ears cause headaches and bad complexions.

Howard also assumes that women are especially subject to nervous diseases. The nerves are destroyed by exercising or working when not inclined, he says, but (in an unconscious paradox) adds that developing willpower depends on healthy nerves. And willpower, of course, is "the rudder of life." Therefore, Howard provides some advice about maintaining healthy nerves: "Sleep always alone. Sleeping with another person is unsanitary. Don't use coffee to overcome fatigue. Shouting and yelling exhaust the nervous powers. Never drink nerve tonics such as 'Dopie' or 'Bromo Tonic.' " We are inclined to agree when he says "Most of the bottled drinks sold at five cents should be thrown into the sewers, and how many diseased lips do you think have touched the glasses passed around at the circus and similar shows?" A final word of advice on this topic suggests that Freud's ideas were beginning to have a wide impact by 1911 (even on working-class girls): "You have heard much about psychotherapy, suggestion and a lot about certain Movements in church circles" as a cure for nerves. A better practice for healthy nerves would be to examine the inner self daily at home.

Uncongenial as it may be to present-day readers, *Confidential Chats with Girls* probably reflects better the daily realities of life at the turn of the century than the more polite and restrained books written for the middle class. Howard's closing chapter of miscellaneous health advice is particularly revealing: Don't giggle—it distorts the face. Don't hold hat pins or theater tickets in the mouth, or use the teeth to pull off glove fingers—there is danger of contracting consumption from such unsanitary habits. Using arsenic to plump up the face is not recommended. And it probably is not very healthy to eat candies with cocaine in them.

A similar attitude of distaste toward feminine and masculine sexuality is evident in Irving David Steinhardt's *Ten Sex Talks to Girls*
and *Ten Sex Talks to Boys* (both 1914), which were based on a lec-
ture series the author had delivered to the Hebrew Educational Society of Brooklyn and the Emanu-El Brotherhood of New York. A
respected member of society, Steinhardt was on the faculty of Cor-
nell University Medical School and had worked with a clinic for
delinquent girls. Like most contemporary sex educators, he was a
member of the American Society of Sanitary and Moral Prophylaxis.
Yet Steinhardt's finickiness seems old-fashioned even for 1914. The
ways of female masturbation, he declaims, are "too disgusting for
utterance." A girl who indulges in excessive self-abuse will end her
days in an insane asylum or in an early grave. Even excessive sexual
indulgence in marriage can lead to such unhappy endings. In a passage extraordinary for the time in its veiled references to lesbian seduction, he warns against overaffectionate girlfriends. A young girl
should avoid a friend who admires her breasts and invites her to stay
overnight or sleep in the same bed. If a girl does accept an invitation
from such a sinister person, she should keep her gown and robe
close around her, beware of snuggling, and ask to sleep in a separate
bed because it is more sanitary. On no account are girls to lie in each
others arms all night and talk about sex.

Steinhardt shows an extreme respect for the physical evidence of
virginity. Douching is not advisable, he maintains, because it might
interfere with the hymen by accident. If a doctor must violate the
hymen he should give the patient a signed statement for her "future
protection against unfounded suspicions." He ends with a warning
against those girls who take pay to bring about the moral ruin of
other girls. "Beware of strange women!" he intones biblically.

In *Ten Sex Talks to Boys*, Steinhardt demonstrates that his misanthropy is not restricted to the female half of the human race. He
begins by justifying sex education in negative terms:

> A criminal silence has been maintained which permitted innumerable
> girls to be morally ruined by the male sex. These girls, as they became
> more and more degraded, likewise became diseased, yet were allowed
> without question or restraints, to ruin the health of their male compan-
> ions. . . .

Steinhardt fills his chapter on male reproductive anatomy with
enough technical detail to discourage anyone but the serious medical student (one illustration, for example, is labeled "Cast of am-
pullae and seminal vesticles, showing winding and sacculation of

lumen"). To further impress the reader with the seriousness of the book, Steinhardt includes exercises at the end of each chapter ("Describe fully the interior of the testicles." "What might produce feeble-mindedness or insanity in children at birth?"). In contrast to the abundant details he supplies in the anatomy section Steinhardt is utterly uninformative on the physiology of coitus:

> All of you should know, and probably do, that children are the result of the proper union of the male and female elements of generation. Also all of you should know, and probably do, that these elements are brought into contact with each other by a certain act or relation which unites the male and the female. This relation is designated as sexual intercourse or the marriage relation, and should never be indulged in before marriage.

This is followed by the declaration, in capital letters, that "THE SEXUAL RELATION IS ABSOLUTELY UNNECESSARY TO YOU OR TO ANY OTHER MAN."

Steinhardt next launches into a recitation of the horrors of venereal disease that is remarkable not only for its lurid detail but also for its persistence even into the 1940 edition: "Seventy to eighty percent of the men who indulge their animal desires are infected with gonorrhea by the fallen women with whom they consort sexually," he begins. The full extent of damage caused by gonorrhea and syphilis is of comparatively recent discovery. In a case of gonorrhea, the primary symptoms cause intense suffering and may lead to abscesses of the bladder, kidney, and prostate and testicles, or even to gonorrheal rheumatism, causing "the most excruciating continuous pain that can be imagined." The end result may be sterilization, blindness, or the deaths of innocent loved ones. Steinhardt invites readers to imagine a tiny grave and tombstone with this pathetic inscription: "Here lies a little blind baby, so afflicted from birth, offered up by its father as a sacrifice to his pre-marriage sacrilege of the sexual relation."

Steinhardt refuses to discuss methods of treatment: "It would only harm you were I to recommend specific modes of treatment. There are many kinds of treatment, and none of them has any place in my talks." Far better to guard against contracting the disease in the first place through sexual abstinence. Never sit on a toilet seat without cleaning it and covering it with paper; never wear other people's clothing, especially rented bathing suits; never swim nude in indoor pools, don't drink alcohol, read licentious matter, or dance. In other words, says Steinhardt, "Just be a real man!"

Having finished with gonorrhea, Steinhardt gives equal attention to the ravages of syphilis. He describes the five types of syphilitic chancres in full detail, while affecting an inability to convey the full horror of the disease:

> To tell you what follows during the acute and chronic stages of this most horrible of diseases is to commence with the hair on the top of the head, to go down to the soles of the feet, and to include every part of the head, body and extremities lying between. . . .

Nevertheless, he steels himself for the challenge ("It will do no harm to touch upon these sequels") and commences the parade of horrors from head to toe, emphasizing again that not only the transgressor is affected: "The sowing of wild oats in the spring-time of youth can make a man later on the murderer of his own child." Steinhardt punctuates his argument by including a photograph of a hideously deformed syphilitic baby, probably a corpse.

By this time, the shaken reader is in a frame of mind to pay strict attention to the author's instructions on disease prevention. Most important, lead a moral life, says Steinhardt. Avoid common drinking cups and towels, shaving brushes and mugs, and all unnecessary physical contact with other people. If one should contract syphilis and have to submit to two years of cure, he should not consider himself clean until he has had negative Wasserman tests from three different doctors. There should be laws, Steinhardt says (and there soon were), requiring Wasserman tests before marriage and the application of silver nitrate to the eyes of newborn babies to be sure they are not afflicted with gonorrhea (which can be passed from mother to child during birth).

Having expended most of this thunder in the chapters on venereal disease, Steinhardt is relatively mild on the subject of masturbation. He suggests that the harm of this practice is psychological rather than physical. It is unhealthy, he says. Being a solitary activity, it can be done to excess, because some masturbators lose the desire for sex with a partner, and because deception about it leads to dishonesty in other areas, too. But after this restrained and modern-sounding passage, he ends the chapter with a reference to masturbatory insanity.

Steinhardt concludes *Ten Sex Talks to Boys* by offering the young male some encouragement and instruction on appropriate attitudes and action toward womankind. He deplores the "freakishness and immodesty" of fashionable female dress, and suggests a remedy:

> We want them [women] to understand that, while not posing as their masters or "bosses," we still have ideas as to what is right and wrong;

and, being convinced of the justness of our ideas, we expect them to conform to these. Certainly our wishes should have as much weight with our women as the dictates of a so-called style.

The young man should keep a tight eye on his female sibling: "Take enough interest in your sister to ascertain where and for whom she works, if she is so unfortunate as to be compelled to go outside of her home to make a livelihood." In that event, he should check his sister's wardrobe frequently to make sure it contains no items suspiciously beyond the reach of her salary. Even toward his fiancee he should be cautious about physical contact, because "kissing in couples is always dangerous" and spreads tuberculosis, syphilis, and other diseases.

Just before World War I, in stark contrast to works like Howard's and Steinhardt's, a few books began to appear that attempted a less didactic and more scientific (though not necessarily more successful) approach to sex education. A particularly unsavory example of this type of book is *My Birth; The Autobiography of an Unborn Infant* (1916) by Armenouhie T. Lamson. In sentimental and breathless prose, the fetus tells the story of its development from conception to the moment before it "appears on the stage of life." Not only is the fetus given a voice but also every cell and organ it encounters speaks and has its own personality and point of view. The overall effect is reminiscent of an utterly humorless cartoon script. Here, for instance, is the ovum describing her meeting with the sperm (how he got there in the first place is carefully ignored). The scene is the fallopian tube:

> As it was very dark and very close about me, I was sure my end was at hand. But then I suddenly felt myself forcefully held and lovingly embraced by a friendly little stranger known as the male germ cell or "Spermatozoon"—during which act the male element disappeared within my body.

A more successful attempt at scientific objectivity is found in Bertha Louise Cady's *The Way Life Begins; An Introduction to Sex Education*. First published in 1917, it was reissued with few changes in 1939. Cady's stated intent is to teach "the deeper meaning of nature study" by examining the reproductive biology of plants and animals in successive chapters on the lily, the moth, the fish, the frog, the chick, the rabbit, and the child. Only the final chapter attempts to address "the personal problems of life." The illustrations are handsome; color plates (hand-colored and pasted in the 1917 edition) depict "sphinx moths gathering nectar from the lily flower," "the life story of the frog," "a nest of newly-born cottontails under cabbage leaves," and, later, the human embryo and the reproductive organs of the male and the female (these last color pictures often have been torn out of extant copies of the work). The information is presented simply and with scientific accuracy, although Cady makes no attempt to move past biological description or to deal with coitus in any terms—physical, psychological, or social. In the last chapter, she asserts that knowledge is the key to right living and self-control, and ignorance creates disharmony, disillusionment, pain, and misery (meaning vice, as Sylvanus Stall had maintained twenty years earlier). Cady's inclusion of this last section is clearly obligatory, however, and incidental to the main purpose of her work. Apart from their relative flaws and their differences in style and content, both Cady's and Lamson's books foreshadow later attempts to separate the presentation of biological information from moralizing discussions of character and sexual conduct.

## The Rosy Girls

Even as the post-Victorian era of sexual repression began to wane, many books written for girls continued to follow the model that had been set by Mary Wood-Allen almost twenty years earlier. There were marginal differences in emphasis, as in Nellie M. Smith's book, *The Three Gifts of Life; A Girl's Responsibility for Race Progress* (1913), which stressed the ability of girls to contribute to the betterment of humanity by selecting husbands with superior genetic and behavioral characteristics. Rose Woodallen Chapman, the daughter of Mary Wood-Allen, also followed her mother's model. She succeeded Wood-Allen as national superintendent of the Purity Department of the Women's Christian Temperance Union, taking office in 1908, the year of her mother's death. From 1910 to 1913 Chapman wrote a popular sex education column for the *Ladies' Home Journal* called "What Shall We Tell the Children?" and in her later years she held office as field secretary of women's work for the American Social Hygiene Association.

Although, like her mother, Chapman enjoyed a wide and responsive readership, her advice tended to be somewhat cautious and prudish in contrast to Wood-Allen's relatively forthright and definite approach. Chapman's *In Her Teens* (1914) warns that the first step on the road of danger can be such "innocent" pleasures as holding hands or allowing an arm about the waist or a goodnight kiss. She quotes from her fan mail: "Some girls write to me that they are so afraid of young men, since hearing of the dangers that exist for girls, that they can hardly speak to them." Goodness, no, says Chapman, she didn't mean to give that impression. A girl need not fear men if she is master of herself. But remember, "no one ever touched another's soul by becoming the plaything of his senses." Despite her exaggerated conservatism, however, Chapman shared the warmth, dedication, and real concern for her young readers that had distinguished her mother's work.

Gradually, however, the works of many sex educators began to show signs of changing times, even as they remained within the Wood-Allen tradition. *The Changing Girl; A Little Book for the Girl of Ten to Fifteen* (1913) by Caroline Wormeley Latimer is unusual in its acknowledgment of female sexuality. Latimer was an instructor in biology at Goucher College and was ahead of her time in conjecturing that "the apparent absence of sex instinct in girls is largely a matter of training extending over many generations." Other writers seemed to alter the pattern almost unconsciously. Mary Gould Hood's *For Girls and the Mothers of Girls* (1914), for example, is a fulsome tract on the pleasures of self-sacrifice and the joys of motherhood, and probably was written in reaction to feminist calls for new freedoms. However, Hood's book stands apart from its predecessors in that it contains the first clinically accurate (if strangely disembodied) description of coitus ever offered in print to girls: "This muscular tube [the penis] deposits the semen in the upper part of the vagina, where the sperm can readily reach the ovum. Such union of the sexes is commonly called intercourse."

As the war years approached, there were frequent references to proper feminine conduct at the office, reflecting the new acceptance of the working woman. Dating, too, began to be mentioned, although with disapproval. *Preparing for Womanhood* (1918) by Edith Belle Lowry illustrates contemporary attempts to reconcile these emerging social patterns with inherited attitudes.

Lowry, a physician, had previously written several sex education books, including *Truths; Talks with a Boy Concerning Himself* (1911) and *Confidences; Talks with a Young Girl Concerning Herself* (1910), which her publisher had promoted as "the only series of books on sex hygiene which has received the endorsement of the leading medical, educational and religious authorities." Addressed to girls aged fifteen to twenty-one, *Preparing for Womanhood* consists mostly of the usual advice on health, recreation, and personal appearance, with an emphasis on the need for girls to learn home-making skills. Lowry includes an unusual feature, however—an entire chapter on the special problems of women in business: "Times have changed greatly, and the girl of today, besides being independent, is a dominant factor in the life of this country and most notably in the cities, where the women not only sway the business world but even the sacred world of politics."

Evidently feeling the need to justify this new role, Lowry explains that a knowledge of business methods enables a girl to run a home better. Furthermore, it is wise for women to prepare for a career in case their husbands die or they encounter "sudden financial misfortune." Paradoxically, she then makes the accusation that many girls do not succeed in the business world because they do not take their work seriously and are only waiting to get married. The girl who wants to do well, says Lowry, should not be afraid to start at the bottom and to do menial chores like dusting the office in addition to her regular duties. She should also be careful to dress modestly and inconspicuously.

Lowry was well aware of the demanding conditions under which most working women labored. A twelve- to sixteen-hour day was not unusual (although New York State had passed "an enlightened law" in 1912 limiting women to a nine-hour workday). Average wages were six dollars a week, but a diligent girl might hope for eventual raises to ten dollars. Lowry deplores the fact that after paying rent and laundry, many working girls have very little left for food, but her advice is less than helpful. "The only solution of this problem that I can see is for each girl to pause and plan her future course carefully."

In a number of other less obvious ways, *Preparing for Womanhood* incorporates and yet departs from the common repertoire of advice to young women. Lowry, for instance, feels that the corset is not so bad after all: "I believe that a large percentage of the objections to the corset originated from women wearing improperly fitted corsets which pushed the organs out of place. A corset fitted to the wearer is not injurious and often serves as a support."

She describes the female reproductive organs in terms of their use by a fetus, not the owner; the uterus is the baby's nest and the vagina is its birth channel. Although she gives the usual cautions against cold, bathing, and exercise during the menstrual period, Lowry excuses girls living away from home from the onerous task of washing out pads made of old rags. (Disposable commercial napkins were not yet available.) She recommends "absorbent cotton enclosed in a thickness of gauze" as an alternative, because these "may be burned instead of laundered."

However conventional, Lowry's discussion of correct behavior for women while in the company of men reflects the emergence of the new pattern of courtship called dating. In particular, she warns against meeting young men at "the corner drugstore"; properly a girl should be called for at her home. Furthermore, girls should dress modestly and bear in mind always that "a man who seeks to destroy your chastity under the guise of love only is cloaking selfish passion under the raiment of affection."

While other writers also attempted to address the practical problems of contemporary girls, Lowry's warning to girls to ignore evident changes in sexual morality and conduct is more representative of the current literature. Indeed, similar cautions in other books for girls from this period constitute the primary evidence that a trend toward sexual freedom in the coming decade was underway. A particularly reactionary example is a pamphlet titled *Why the Roses Bloom; A Message to Girls,* written about 1919 and attributed to Sina Stratton, superintendent of moral education for the Women's Christian Temperance Union. A labored metaphor of the young girl as a newly opened rose runs throughout its twenty-three pages ("Your individual rose is finished, the perfect bloom of womanhood has come . . ."). The explanation of "why the roses bloom" is, of course, those vital bodily fluids, which are held in reserve in

> two little store rooms called ovaries. From their very substance a fluid is thrown into your blood, which recreates you, physically, mentally, spiritually and causes you to grow rounded and have color in your cheeks. God wants to use this fluid which is being poured into your bloodstream, to recreate you into the perfect woman, before there can be any surplus, to create through you, that second individual, your child, your rose. It is this creative force in you, that if rightly used, will enable you to go through your school and college work with credit, and after you leave, to make a success of whatever line of work you may select.

Every girl should be alert to protect her bloom from the hazards of loose behavior. Girls must not tempt men, Stratton says in a passage foreshadowing the image of the "flaming youth" of the twenties, by meeting them for "dates" or at the "movies," or by dressing indecently, bleaching their hair, painting or powdering, or taking part in promiscuous fondling and kissing. "Indulgence in these liberties, and thus catering to, and arousing this sex instinct, outside the marriage vows, leads to many a clandestine mating, and many an unwelcome child is born to a life of sin." Such behavior, or even solitary vice in the form of prurient thoughts, can interfere with development. The sad result can be colorless cheeks where no roses bloom and which must be painted to simulate the real blossoming of God's purpose.

As we shall see in the next chapter, from the same generation of sex educators who continued to reassert the function of motherhood as "God's purpose" for women, rose a few impassioned activists who challenged the very core of this argument.

## BIBLIOGRAPHY

Bisseker, H. *When a Boy Becomes a Man; A Little Book for Boys.* Edward Bok Books of Self-Knowledge for Young People and Parents, vol. 2. New York: Fleming H. Revell Co., 1912.

Boy Scouts of America. *Official Handbook for Boys.* New York: Doubleday, Page, and Co., 1911.

Cady, Bertha Louise (Chapman). *The Way Life Begins; An Introduction to Sex Education.* New York: American Social Hygiene Association, 1917; rev. ed., 1939.

Chapman, Rose Woodallen. *In Her Teens.* New York: Fleming H. Revell Co., 1914.

Foster, William Trufant, ed. *The Social Emergency; Studies in Sex Hygiene and Morals.* Boston: Houghton Mifflin, 1914.

Hall, Winfield Scott. *Father and Son; John's Vacation; What John Saw in the Country.* Chicago: American Medical Association Press, 1913.

———. *From Youth into Manhood.* New York: Young Men's Christian Association Press, 1909.

———. *Margaret, The Doctor's Daughter.* Sex Education Pamphlets. Chicago: American Medical Association, 1911.

Hood, Mary Gould. *For Girls and the Mothers of Girls; A Book for the Home and the School concerning the Beginnings of Life.* Indianapolis: Bobbs-Merrill Co., 1914.

Howard, William Lee. *Confidential Chats with Girls.* New York: E. J. Clode, 1911.

King, Elisha Alonzo. *Helps to Health and Purity.* Des Moines, IA: Personal Help Publishing Co., 1903.

———. *A Talk to Men.* Des Moines, IA: Personal Help Publishing Co., 1897.

———, and Meyer, F. B. *Clean and Strong.* Boston: United Society of Christian Endeavor, 1909; rev. ed., 1917.

Lamson, Armenouhie T. (Tashjian). *My Birth; The Autobiography of an Unborn Infant.* New York: Macmillan, 1916.

Latimer, Caroline Wormeley. *The Changing Girl; A Little Book for the Girl of Ten to Fifteen.* Edward Bok Books of Self-Knowledge for Young People and Parents, no. 5. New York: Fleming H. Revell Co., 1913.

Lowry, Edith Belle. *Confidences; Talks with a Young Girl Concerning Herself.* Chicago: Forbes and Co., 1910.

————. *Preparing for Womanhood*. Chicago: Forbes and Co., 1918.

————. *Truths; Talks with a Boy Concerning Himself*. Chicago: Forbes and Co., 1911.

Moore, Harry Hascall. *Keeping in Condition; Handbook on Training for Older Boys*. New York: Macmillan, 1916.

Smith, Nellie May. *The Three Gifts of Life; A Girl's Responsibility for Race Progress*. New York: Dodd, Mead and Co., 1913.

Steinhardt, Irving David. *Ten Sex Talks to Boys*. Philadelphia: Lippincott, 1914.

————. *Ten Sex Talks to Girls*. Philadelphia: Lippincott, 1914.

Stratton, Sina. *Why the Roses Bloom; A Message to Girls*. Philadelphia: Women's Christian Temperance Union, 1919?

Wile, Ira Solomon. *Sex Education*. New York: Duffield and Co., 1912.

# 4
# *Two Trials*

Since the appearance of the earliest examples of the genre in the 1890s up to the present day, most sex education books written for young adults have enjoyed warm approval from mainstream thinkers of their era. The books nearly always accurately reflect, or even lag a bit behind, the accepted sexual ideas of their time; if a title sells at all well, it is likely to go through several editions at short intervals in which minor adjustments are made to bring it abreast of the shifts in public sexual opinion. In the past eight decades there have been only two major obscenity trials involving an adolescent sex education book. In both these cases the obscenity charges were only an excuse for a political vendetta against the authors. The real issue was the legality of birth control, and the targets of official wrath were Margaret Sanger in 1916 and Mary Ware Dennett in 1929. Both were prosecuted under the notorious Comstock Law, which prohibited the distribution of contraception information and any other "obscene" material through the United States mails.

## "What Every Girl Should Know"

Margaret Higgins Sanger first became aware of the legal restraints on the distribution of contraception information as an outgrowth of her work as a nurse in the slums of New York City in the early 1900s. Having "asked doctors what one could do" to circumvent the bans, she learned (as she relates in *My Fight for Birth Control*) that "I'd better keep off that subject or Anthony Comstock would get me." Later, after she had indeed been "got" by Comstock, she was to refer to him as "that flamboyant and pathological zealot." Comstock's life merited both adjectives. He brought a wild-eyed energy and enthusiasm to the abolishment of obscenity, which he defined in terms of

**53**

his personal aversions and which he saw everywhere. In his book *Traps for the Young*, written in 1883, he revealed a vision of contemporary America in which vice spread and ensnared the young through newspapers, books, advertisements, classic literature, and almost every other form of human communication.

Comstock had been a powerful figure for forty years before he clashed with Sanger. In 1872, when he was 28 years old and a private citizen living in Brooklyn, New York, Comstock became an officer of an antivice committee of the Young Men's Christian Association (the committee that in 1875 became the New York Society for the Suppression of Vice, which supported Comstock's censorship activities throughout his career). With this official backing he went to Washington and lobbied vigorously for the passage of an antiobscenity bill he had written, and succeeded in ramming it through an inattentive Congress at the closing session of March 1873.

Amended and slightly reworded in 1876, the Comstock Law forbade the dissemination through the U.S. Post Office of "every obscene, lewd, lascivious, indecent, filthy or vile" object or publication, as well as any object or publication "intended for preventing conception or producing abortion, or for any indecent or immoral use." This law, which was subsequently reclassified from the Post Office Code (Section 211) to the criminal section of the U.S. Code (Title 18, Sections 1461-1462), declared such materials "nonmailable" and allowed for the punishment of offenders through fine, imprisonment, or both.

Shortly after the bill was passed, Comstock was commissioned a special agent (solicitor) of the post office to see that the law was enforced. Supported by the law and the authority of his position, Comstock quickly assumed the role of public censor. Working at both national and local levels (the Comstock Law opened the way for the passage of numerous state laws prohibiting the publication, sale, and distribution of obscene matter and information about abortion and contraception), Comstock was unimpeded in effecting the suppression of any material he considered "unmailable." By the time of his death in 1915, he had made 1,792 arrests and seized 45 tons of obscene matter.

Margaret Sanger was equally zealous in devotion to her own cause—birth control, a term she claimed to have coined herself. In her *Autobiography* (1938) and in *My Fight for Birth Control* (1931), she tells of her harsh childhood as one of eleven children and of her mother's premature death at age forty-eight. Born in 1883 in Corning,

New York, she was married in 1900 to architect William Sanger. In 1912 the couple moved to Manhattan where their home soon became a gathering place for intellectuals and activists of the left—socialists, anarchists, and wobblies—and where Margaret's work in the Lower East Side further exposed her to the suffering caused by unlimited breeding in poverty.

One night that year she was asked by a socialist friend to fill in for a speaker at a meeting for working women. Out of that speech Sanger developed a series of articles called *What Every Girl Should Know* for the radical newspaper, the *Call*. When the paper announced that one of the final installments in the series would discuss venereal disease, it was informed by the Post Office Department, led by Comstock, that the paper's mailing permit would be revoked if it attempted to include the article. Faced with this ultimatum, the *Call* printed the ironic caption "What Every Girl Should Know—Nothing!" in place of the suppressed article. Undeterred by the brush with censorship, Sanger had the full series printed and distributed as a pamphlet in 1914.

Dedicated to "the working girls of the world," *What Every Girl Should Know* is characterized by a straightforward style and a burning concern for women's rights. After detailed descriptions of the male and female sexual anatomy, conception, and birth (with a diagram of the female internal genitalia), Sanger discusses the delicate mental state of the pubescent girl and proposes that the nervous strain of menstruation would be relieved if working women banded together and demanded one day's rest a month during their periods. Even more radical, Sanger dares to hint that unmarried motherhood may be an enriching experience, and that "women should know that creative energy does not need to be expended entirely on the propagation of the race." She defines the difference between the young male and female sexual impulse in these terms: girls desire to touch, caress, and speak to the opposite sex; boys desire to discharge the accumulation of sex cells and relieve nervous tension. Masturbation is a habit that is easily acquired by girls as well as boys, and girls who do it may (in a ground-breaking but oblique first reference to female orgasm) "find themselves incapable of any relief in the natural act, tossing about nervously for hours after."

Convinced that "in Anglo-Saxon women the sex desire is latent until the age of thirty," Sanger refers to this as an advantage in that it allows women to sublimate their energies into "the bigger and broader movements and activities in which they are active today." In a section on pregnancy, she enumerates the dangers of abortion and induced miscarriages, and gives the symptoms and duration of gestation. She expresses conventional views on the theory of seminal power, and denies the myth that sex is necessary for health, but the double standard reaps her scorn: "Every girl should look upon the man who indulges freely in sexual relations without social responsibility, as a prostitute far more degraded than the unfortunate girl compelled to sell her body to sustain life."

Sanger is indignant at the number of wives who are infected with venereal diseases by their libertine husbands: "Three out of every five married women in New York have gonorrhea." Further, "if women voluntarily exposed themselves to diseases which sapped the husband's vitality, making him a dependent invalid or exposed him to the shock of a mutilating operation, or death—would men continue to suffer?" In the section objected to by the postal authorities, Sanger gives the symptomatology and means of transmission of syphilis, and deplores the difficulties for working people in obtaining treatment. Only in the later editions (the pamphlet was reissued in 1927 under the title *What Every Boy and Girl Should Know*) did Sanger conclude this work with a veiled reference to birth control: "Stop bringing to birth children whose inheritance cannot be one of health or intelligence. Stop bringing into the world children whose parents cannot provide for them. Herein lies the key of civilization." An advertisement on the last page announced that "Socialist Party Locals, Branches, and dealers can obtain this book at the following prices. . . ."

Also in 1914, Sanger began to edit a periodical, the *Woman Rebel*, in which she published articles advocating sexual freedom for women and closely skirting the birth control issue. This, too, was declared unmailable, but Sanger continued to publish it in spite of repeated warnings from the Post Office Department. She was soon in serious trouble with the law, and in late 1914 was forced to flee to Europe to gain time to prepare a legal defense against charges of obscenity. It was during this period of exile that she became the friend and admirer of Havelock Ellis, whose theories on the spiritual and emotional aspects of sex left a deep impression on her, and met the British birth control advocate Dr. Marie Stopes. (Stopes was then writing *Married Love*, which was vigorously banned in the United States following its publication in 1918.)

Meantime, Comstock sent a decoy to William Sanger's home to buy a copy of Margaret's pamphlet *Family Limitation* (1915), a practical guide to birth control methods that Margaret had arranged to have distributed in her absence. Comstock personally arrested William Sanger the next day. The game was for high stakes: Comstock offered William acquittal in exchange for information about Margaret's whereabouts. Indignantly refusing, Sanger asked Comstock what he would consider appropriate punishment for the author of the pamphlet. "Five years hard labor for every copy printed!" he snapped. Within the year William was tried and found guilty of distributing obscene literature, and subsequently served thirty days in jail.

Soon after William's trial in September 1915, Margaret returned voluntarily for her own trial. She found that in her absence a National Birth Control League had been formed, and had been given her files and mailing lists. Meeting with this group, she was astounded to be told by its president, Mary Ware Dennett, that the league could not support her illegal methods because it was committed to changing the laws in an orderly and proper manner, rather than defying them. But public opinion had grown in favor of Sanger during her year's absence and the league reversed its opinion just before the trial. Furthermore, Margaret was no longer faced with the personal opposition of Anthony Comstock, who had died (after catching a chill at William Sanger's trial), and when Margaret's case came to trial in February 1916, it was immediately dismissed. The postal authorities were not appeased, however, and bided their time.

Turning to more concrete action later that year, Margaret opened a birth control clinic in the Brownsville section of Brooklyn in a working-class neighborhood. Assisted by her sister, Ethel Byrne, and a young friend, Fania Mindell, she worked from morning until night fitting diaphragms and giving birth control information to the women who flocked to the clinic for help. Margaret's venture was in direct opposition to New York State laws, which said that only doctors could prescribe contraceptive devices and only for the cure or prevention of disease. It was not long before the police arrived. All three women were arrested. Margaret was charged with conducting a birth control clinic; Ethel, with disseminating birth control information; and Fania Mindell, with selling an indecent publication—*What Every Girl Should Know.*

Amid lurid press coverage and deafening public outcry, Ethel was convicted and nearly died in prison on a hunger strike. Fania Mindell was convicted and fined $50, later reversed on appeal. Sanger, also found guilty, was sent to prison for thirty days and although she, too, appealed her case, her conviction was upheld. However, the judge who heard Sanger's appeal significantly altered the interpretation of the state statute regarding the prescription of contraceptives for the cure or prevention of disease (previously understood to mean venereal disease only); he allowed that a doctor could give contraceptive advice to any married woman who required it for the maintenance of her health. On the strength of this decision, Margaret reopened her birth control clinic in Manhattan in 1923, paving the way for the establishment of numerous other clinics across the country.

In succeeding years, Sanger wrote and lectured widely on birth control. At one point she noted ironically that "the section on venereal disease in *What Every Girl Should Know,* which had once been banned in the New York *Call* and for which Fania had been fined, was now, officially but without credit, reprinted and distributed among the soldiers going into cantonments and abroad." Before her death in 1966, Sanger saw the fulfillment of many of her dreams for liberalized access to birth control information. However, it was not until 1971 that the Comstock Law was modified to allow the mailing of contraceptives and birth control information to the general public.

## "The Sex Side of Life"

In one of history's minor ironies, Mary Ware Dennett, the president of the National Birth Control League who had self-righteously refused support for Sanger's illegal methods, in 1929 found herself the defendant in the second obscenity trial of an adolescent sex education book. The testimony and evidence in the case are recorded in detail and with considerable emotion by Dennett in her book *Who's Obscene?* (1930), written immediately after the trial. Although it is clear that the real matter at issue was her political activities on behalf of birth control, the nature of the testimony is an interesting commentary on the state of sex education literature in 1929.

The title accused of obscenity was a slight pamphlet of only twenty-one pages—*The Sex Side of Life* (1918). Dennett wrote the pamphlet for her own two boys, aged eleven and fourteen, "after examining about sixty publications on the subject and forming the opinion that they were inadequate and unsatisfactory." "I found none," she explains, "that I was willing to put into their hands without first guarding them against what I considered very misleading and harmful impressions." And so she set out to write her own book.

In Dennett's opinion, her work differed from that which had gone before in several important respects. First, she used "proper terminology" in calling things by their right scientific names. She emphasized the unlikeness of human reproduction to that of plants and animals and she was honest in saying that venereal disease was becoming curable.

But the most significant difference in her mind, and in the minds of the hostile witnesses at the trial, was the fact that she dealt with what she called "the emotional side of life." As she explained, "in not a single one of all the books for young people that I have thus far read has there been the frank and unashamed declaration that the climax of sex emotion is an unsurpassed joy." And so Dennett said the unsayable—she told young people that sex was pleasurable. The passage in question, while it probably would not have provoked a censorship attempt had it not been for the political issue, is a more explicit description of coitus than anything that had ever before been offered to adolescents:

> When a man and a woman fall in love so that they really belong to each other, the physical side of the relation is this: both of them feel at intervals a peculiar thrill or glow, particularly in the sexual organs, and it naturally culminates after they have gone to bed at night. The man's special sex organ or penis, becomes enlarged and stiffened, instead of soft and limp as ordinarily, and thus it easily enters the passage in the woman's body called the vagina or birth-canal, which leads to the uterus or womb, which as perhaps you already know is the sac in which the egg or embryo grows into a baby. The penis and the vagina are about the same size, as Nature intended them to fit each other. By a rhythmic movement of the penis in and out, the sex act reaches an exciting climax or orgasm, when there is for the woman a peculiarly satisfying contraction of the muscles of the passage and for the man, the expulsion of the semen, the liquid which contains the germs of life. This is followed by a sensation of peaceful happiness and sleepy relaxation. It is the very greatest physical pleasure to be had in all human experience, and it helps very much to increase all other kinds of pleasure also. It is at this time that married people not only are closest to each other physically, but they feel closer to each other in every other way, too.

The large part of the pamphlet is taken up with physiological descriptions related to the two very clear drawings by Dr. Robert L. Dickinson showing the male and female internal reproductive systems. Dennett explains the mechanics of conception and birth briefly, and laments "at present, unfortunately, it is against the law to give people information as to how to manage their sex relations so that no baby will be created unless the father and mother are ready and glad to have it happen." About masturbation she says, "Recently many of the best scientists have concluded that the chief harm has come from the worry caused by doing it. There is no occasion for worry unless the habit is carried to excess," but the young person should not yield to the impulse unless the pressure is overwhelming. Dennett concludes with a warning against venereal disease and prostitution, and praise for sex relations between people who love each other.

Dennett's essay was first printed privately, then in the *Medical Review of Reviews* for February 1918, and finally produced as a pamphlet and sold for twenty-five cents through the mails to meet a growing demand. The venture was distinctly secondary for Dennett, however; the main part of her attention and energies was taken up with her activities as director of the Voluntary Parenthood League. In the years 1919 and 1920 those activities took the form of a survey of Congress to find a sponsor for a bill to remove the words "preventing conception" from the Comstock Law. In 1921 the league was given new hope by the appointment of William Hays as postmaster general. Hays was vociferous in repudiating the role of censor in his new job, but, unfortunately, soon resigned to work with the censorship problems of the movie industry. His successor, Hubert Work, vigorously supported the obscenity laws and lost no time in issuing bulletins to that effect to local post offices. Sorely disappointed, Dennett wrote a steamy editorial for the *Birth Control Herald* in July 1922, attacking Work's stand. Two months later she was informed by the solicitor of the Post Office (the position held for so many years by Comstock) that *The Sex Side of Life* had been declared unmailable. Dennett ignored this decree, and continued to meet the demand for copies through the mails.

By 1925, public acclaim for the pamphlet had grown to such proportions that Dennett asked some of the most prestigious users for a statement of support. This was submitted to the solicitor with a request that the ban be removed. The Post Office refused. Dennett pressed on, demanding to know which passages were considered obscene, and, in a lengthy correspondence, pushed to know how the Post Office could be aware of the contents of sealed first-class mail. It was a surprise to no one when, in January 1929, she was indicted on charges of mailing obscene matter. The penalty was a maximum fine of $5,000 or five years in jail.

After many postponements, the case was heard in April of that year. The judge, Warren Burrows, charged the jury to determine whether the pamphlet's "language has a tendency to deprave and corrupt the morals of those whose minds are open to such things, arousing and implanting in such minds lewd and obscene thoughts or desires." Defense attorney Morris L. Ernst presented an imposing array of endorsements from twenty scientific, educational, and religious authorities, including John Dewey, representatives from Union Theological Seminary, the YMCA, the YWCA, and the Child Study Association of America. At the judge's request twelve of these witnesses and an equal number of witnesses for the prosecution were invited to submit statements to the court. These letters Dennett later included in *Who's Obscene?*. Those for the defense praised *The Sex Side of Life* as "healthy," "sane," and "wholesome" and many compared it favorably to other pamphlets distributed by educational, religious, or government organizations. Statistical and medical testimony to support Dennett's attitudes about masturbation were provided by several of the medical authorities.

The prosecution, on the other hand, evidently had a hard time rounding up expert witnesses. Only eleven relatively obscure clergymen, doctors, and civil servants could be found who were willing to go on record. Their contributions were not distinguished by moderation. Reverend John Roach Straton, pastor of Calvary Baptist Church of New York, labeled the pamphlet "utterly ruinous in its effect on the young" and "a positive and deadly menace." Dr. Howard Kelly, professor of gynecology at Johns Hopkins University, was even more emphatic: "With one exception the most prurient statement that has come to my notice. . . . Language could not be used more calculated to excite illegitimate, unrestrainable passions than the nasty minutiae upon which Mary Dennett lingers with such obvious unction." Kelly declared that "[Dennett's] contention is absolutely false that women discover any such extreme gratification in their sex relations; many women are and remain utterly indifferent, and their participation is but a matter of complaisance."

The other witnesses for the prosecution were equally disapproving. Their criticism centered on what they considered a "brazen defense" of masturbation, a lack of emphasis on self-control, and the danger of the pamphlet being read by younger children. They felt that Dennett was advocating birth control and that her emphasis on love in sex relations was a negation of marriage and akin to approval of free love. They found the pictures vile, or at least unnecessary. And most of all they objected to the vivid description of intercourse, called it titillating, alluring, and an "unnecessary glorification of the sexual act." They worried that young people reading the passage might be tempted to act it out (an argument that was to resurface in the fifties during the controversy over sex education in the schools). John Sumner, the secretary of the New York Society for the Suppression of Vice, deplored Dennett's revelation of a cure for venereal disease because it minimized the "punishment following sex iniquity." One of the witnesses even stooped to personal attack; New York State Senator William Lathrop Love wrote: "There is also a recital of intimate experiences that give the impression that they were anticipated for a great many years and when finally realized made such an impression on her that she doesn't hesitate in telling the world."

During the trial, prosecutor James E. Wilkinson, who referred to Dennett's pamphlet as "perverted sex instruction," repeatedly blocked evidence showing that the pamphlet had been used in large quantity for ten years by many respectable organizations. A jury of middle-aged and elderly family men found Mary Ware Dennett guilty of mailing an obscene publication. In spite of vociferous objection in the press and many letters asking Judge Burrows to override the verdict, Dennett was sentenced to pay a fine of $300.

The verdict was reversed on appeal by Judge Augustus N. Hand, who wrote "The old theory that information about sex matters should be left to chance has greatly changed. . . . We have been referred to no decision where a truthful exposition of the sex side of life evidently calculated for instruction and for the explanation of relevant facts has been held to be obscene." In a precedent-making decision, he ruled that any tendency to arouse sex impulses was incidental to the main purpose of this sex education pamphlet.

Mary Ware Dennett combated censorship all the rest of her life through the New York Civil Liberties League and the National Council for Freedom from Censorship. At this writing, the Comstock Law still remains a part of the American legal code.

## BIBLIOGRAPHY

Comstock, Anthony. *Traps for the Young*. New York: Funk and Wagnalls, 1883.

Dennett, Mary Ware. *The Sex Side of Life; An Explanation for Young People*. Astoria, NY: Published by the author, 1918.

———. *Who's Obscene?* New York: Vanguard Press, 1930.

Sanger, Margaret. *Family Limitation*. New York: Published by the author, 1915.

———. *Margaret Sanger, An Autobiography*. New York: W. W. Norton, 1938.

———. *My Fight for Birth Control*. New York: Farrar and Rinehart, 1931.

———. *What Every Boy and Girl Should Know*. New York: Brentano's, 1927.

———. *What Every Girl Should Know*. Reading, PA: Sentinel Printing Co., 1914; New York: M. N. Maisel, 1915.

# 5

## *Between the Wars*

During the years between the two world wars, there was a dearth of new sex education books in America. The flood of literature for the young that had been written to assuage Victorian fears dwindled to a trickle as new liberal attitudes toward sex emerged in the twenties. With less urgency to indoctrinate teenagers in sex prevention, fewer books were written. For the conservative minority, many older titles continued in print or were reissued in new editions; the new titles that did appear in this decade and the next tended either to ignore changing patterns of behavior or to warn against them. The purpose of sex education for the young continued to be the prevention, not the encouragement, of sexual behavior.

At the beginning of the decade, Louise Frances Spaller offered *Personal Help for Boys* (1921), which was in the tradition of the "bully boys" books. Spaller had written *Personal Help for Girls* in 1918, but felt, as she explained in her preface, that she had a special rapport with boys: "Hundreds of them have said that I seemed to know how it is with a feller." Typically, Spaller holds up Teddy Roosevelt as an ideal ("He had the grit and willpower to keep up his daily training, and, the result was, he built a weakling of a boy into a giant of a man"). With heavy jocularity and labored spriteliness, she lays out "the fun trail" of pep and bully things to do, extols Scouting as a way to become "a dandy scrapper," and emphasizes camping, outdoor activities, and hobbies ("Betcha life! Gee, it's jake!"). Two of her stories are heavily racist even for that bigoted decade: a description of some "chinks" at a Chinese New Year's celebration, and a tale about an "old darky" who was scared by some boys' ghost tricks, proving, as Spaller explains, that "fear is especially deep-rooted in the ignorant and the negro."

Perhaps feeling some limits to her vaunted rapport with boys, Spaller delegates the actual sex instruction to Professor Thomas W. Shannon, who subsequently wrote a complementary "Personal

**63**

Help" volume for men. In eight short supplementary chapters Shannon tells "The Story of Life." A look at the chapter headings indicates a predictable and derivative approach: "Boys make men," "The story of life among the plants," "The story of life among oysters and fish," "The story of life among insects and birds," "The story of animal and human life," "Strong boys make strong men," "Weak boys make weak men," and "What kind of a boy will you be?" The expected diatribe against masturbation points out that prisons and insane asylum inmates are masturbators, and that a boy who wastes his sex fluids is liable to end up either there or in an early grave. Shannon's only original words are a broadside against tobacco. He describes a scientific experiment in which leeches were applied to the arms of both smokers and nonsmokers. Those that were sucking the blood of smokers soon began to tremble and jerk, and presently fell to the floor dead.

It was books such as Spaller's that prompted Marie Stopes, the influential sex education pioneer, to deplore the whole genre in *Sex and the Young* (1926):

> Almost without exception I must warn teachers against the books at present existing, rather than encourage them to place them in young people's hands. . . . There are now many works professing to give full details which so overload the horrors and dangers of sex experience, prostitution and other evils as really almost to terrify young people about the future awaiting them in their adult life. . . . Lurid warnings and pronouncements about masturbation are best kept away from healthy young people.

Stopes felt that rather than being singled out for special instruction, sex education should be incorporated throughout school curriculums.

A book that has more of the look of the twenties is *Letters to My Daughter* by Leslie J. Swabacker (1926). Modishly printed in art deco style and with a format reminiscent of that of Kahlil Gibran's *The Prophet* (which had been published in 1923), the book consists of letters of advice from a father to his four-year-old daughter in anticipation of her teen years. Swabacker attempts to take a modern, enlightened stance. His writing is sprinkled with Freudian terms—"inhibitions," "repressions," "Electra complex," "the subconscious"—but demonstrates very little comprehension of their meanings. He professes to welcome the new sexual attitudes, but it soon becomes apparent that his real purpose is to keep his daughter a virgin at all costs.

Like *The Prophet,* Swabacker's advice is packaged in sections labeled Religion, Duty, Conduct, Love, Marriage, and so on. In the section on religion, he discourages his daughter from attending church and points out the historical shortcomings of both the Jewish and the Christian traditions; the Golden Rule should be quite enough. As for duty, she should dress well and be loyal to her employer, but be unconcerned about duty to her parents. Smoking, drinking, and dancing are all right since everyone does it, but petting is another matter—"a dangerous game," "a dingy ante-room to passion," and "an open gateway to hell." Honesty is a useful virtue, and lies should be limited to ten a week. Swabacker praises monogamy and, to ensure its preservation, suggests that the art of love and the Kama Sutra be taught in school (although he offers no specifics).

Regarding men, Swabacker warns his daughter that most of them "never miss an opportunity to enjoy any woman they can secure. . . . The game of flirtation is played by different rules by the two sexes." For men, a visit to a prostitute is like a visit to the barber or the chiropodist, while women bring a quality of "emotional longing" to sexual experience. In short, "Preserve your chastity for your husband." In choosing him, she should pick a man no more than three to seven years older than she, to make sure there is no Electra complex involved. He should be her mental equal or superior, physically attractive, with a sense of humor, and should provide her with a doctor's certificate attesting to his being untainted with venereal disease or hereditary insanity and certifying the fact that his "virility is unimpaired."

The engagement should last no more than three months because it is a "time of sweet danger." Due to the unsettling effects of the war and of women's suffrage and liberation, it is "the custom in this year, A.D. 1926, for a great many girls to give themselves completely to their husbands-to-be during this period." However, Swabacker is sure that the pendulum will soon swing back from this extreme. On marriage, he is unenlightening except for the ominous warning that the average bride goes to the marriage bed "with the same feeling that we approach a precipice in the dark." A new husband should be considerate of his bride, and "if he behaves like a beast hit him with a suitcase." And they should both study the art of love to keep enjoyment fresh.

Although they were not sex education books, two titles that much interested young people in these years were *The Revolt of Modern Youth* (1925) and *Companionate Marriage* (1929) by Judge Benjamin Lindsey of the Juvenile and Family Court of Denver. Impressed by the honesty and forthrightness of young people in sexual matters, Judge Lindsey proposed in his books to recodify existing sexual patterns according to his concept of "companionate marriage." As he explained it, "Companionate marriage is legal marriage, with legalized birth control, and with the right to divorce by mutual consent for childless couples, usually without payment of alimony." To bring this about, three bills were needed: to repeal the laws against birth control, to legalize birth control clinics, and to allow divorce by mutual consent. This proposition caused a great stir in Judge Lindsey's time, and it is only now that his ideas are becoming reality.

The sex education book that was undoubtably the most widely read in these years was *Growing Up* by Karl De Schweinitz (1928). Although it is very simply written and was probably intended for third- and fourth-grade children, it appeared frequently in recommended bibliographies for teenagers. The first edition was reprinted fifteen times in the first three years of publication. Its biological approach won great favor in an era that equated "scientific" with "modern" and had the added advantage of making it possible to sidestep psychological and ethical problems.

Although De Schweinitz sticks to the biological facts of conception, fetal development, and birth, without digressing into the topic of correct sexual behavior, he interlaces his clinical descriptions with sentimental prose and coy illustrations. The frontispiece of *Growing Up*, captioned "Out of the everywhere," depicts a chubby and surprised-looking naked baby sitting incongruously on a cliff somewhere in what appears to be the Swiss Alps. A few pages later there are drawings of a calf in the uterus, showing the cow in silhouette, and a human fetus in the uterus (but without a corresponding outline of the woman). Photographs of eggs in the nest, an Easter lily, a butterfly and a phlox, and a drawing of the sperm and egg of a minnow illustrate the chapter on fertilization. A small drawing of a human sperm is tucked in at the bottom of a page. A picture of a lactating sow appears near an Italianate painting of a mother nursing an infant. The structure of the penis and testicles is discreetly illustrated through a snapshot of a male dog sitting up on his haunches. Other examples from the animal kingdom—a German shepard feeding pups, a buffalo calf nursing, a lion cub—lead up to a statue of a nude boy by Alexander Calder appropriately titled "Man Cub." Female nudity is also shown in statuary—a slim, teenage "Bathing Girl." The last chapter, on mating, depicts a bull moose and his mate and reproduces a painting of *Sleeping Beauty* in which round-faced children play at being sweethearts.

The "birds and bees" format of *Growing Up* derives directly from the opening chapters of Sylvanus Stall's *What a Young Boy Ought to Know*. The question is "Where do babies come from?" and the answer is a description of the fertilization arrangements of plants, fish, birds, mammals, and—at last—humans. In its own time *Growing Up* was most similar to Bertha Cady's *The Way Life Begins* (described in Chapter 3), which was first published in 1917, and later reached new popularity in the 1939 edition.

De Schweinitz tackles the facts of conception by generalizing that "everything starts as eggs." To the egg is added the male contribution—pollen, milt, sperm—to add up to the seed or the embryo. The dog, the elephant, the mouse, and other mammals differ from lesser creatures in that the mother has a "nest" for the eggs inside her body and the father has a "tube" through which to pass the sperm safely into the female. In animal mating the penis fits inside the vagina, and the sperm stays in the testicles until it is needed.

This is the way it is for humans beings, too, De Schweinitz explains cautiously: "The father places the sperms in the body of the mother in very much the same way that the four-legged animals do, only the mother and father can lie together facing each other. The penis then fits into the vagina of the mother which has its own opening underneath the opening for the urine or waste water." This passage is typical of a number of oversimplifications in *Growing Up* that could have led to some serious misinterpretation by young readers. (This author can attest to the confusing effect of this particular description of coitus, having been given De Schweinitz to read at age ten. The book's joyless and clinical tone led to the impression that sexual intercourse was a medical procedure.)

In another passage, De Schweinitz suggests that conception is an inevitable result of every sexual encounter; and, at the same time, he fails to take advantage of the opportunity to describe menstruation: "If no sperms have been sent to meet it, the egg stays in the uterus for a little while and then passes out through the vagina." De Schweinitz's oversimplified approach blithely ignores the whole problem of sexual ethics: "Like the animals a man and a woman may feel like sending the sperm to join the egg but they do not do this unless they love each other."

The final chapter lapses into rhapsodic praise of mating throughout nature. The flowers in spring are "dressed as if to welcome the tiny visitors who carry the pollen from flower to flower." From this lowly example to the mystery of human love, attraction between male and female is the source of beauty in the world.

Many of the shortcomings of *Growing Up* probably result from the fact that it was intended for much younger children than its eventual readership. Although the lack of moralizing in De Schweinitz's book is refreshing when compared to its predecessors, it is difficult to imagine that its bare biological facts and sentimentalities offered much help to a teenager trying to manage a nascent sexuality.*

Some old favorites appeared during the decade in new editions that showed only token attempts at modernization. Margaret Sanger rewrote *What Every Girl Should Know* in 1927 to reach a broader audience with a new title *What Every Boy and Girl Should Know.* In 1926 Armenouhie Lamson updated *How I Came to Be* by removing some of the sillier personifications (the fetus is no longer "embarrassed" by its tail) and by adding a chapter on evolution as re-created in the growth of the embryo. In 1924, Harry Hascall Moore's *Keeping in Condition* reappeared almost unchanged. *What a Young Boy Ought to Know* was tentatively reissued in 1926. (Although Stall had died in 1915, no new name appears on the title page as author of the revision. However, the copyright is attributed to Fannie C. Cash.) Evidently well received, the book was reprinted two years later when the other seven volumes of the Self and Sex series were also issued in new editions.

*Young Boy* remained almost unchanged, with all of its Victorian prose on the horrid effects of masturbation nearly intact. *Young Man,* however, was rewritten in "bully boy" style, although the message remained the same. The revised version puts heavy emphasis on business success as proof (or result) of manhood, using such inspirational slogans as "Be a human flashlight!" and "Avoid a heavy stomach and a cloudy brain!" In an economic metaphor, Cash points out the high cost of low living—"this world should be run for the decent and decency; this world must not be run for the nasty." She extols exercise, continence, and clean living and deplores venereal disease, whose symptoms she describes vividly but ungrammatically as "the abscesses that fill the liver, turns the kidneys into gristle and rottens the bones." However, the book is still very much Stall's

---

*The British edition of *Growing Up,* published in 1931 by Routledge and Sons, has some notable omissions. It leaves out the dog sitting up on its haunches, the nude female statue (but not the male), and the two sentences describing coitus.

own as evidenced in the last chapters that discuss such topics as "The appalling penalties exacted by vice" and "Lost manhood and how to regain it."

# The Reaction against "Modern Liberties"

While sex instruction in the twenties largely ignored the upheavals in sexual behavior patterns that characterized the decade, the books of the thirties began to show a reaction to the new freedoms. Although sex educators of that decade were careful to disassociate themselves from the Victorian horror stories about masturbation, they focused sharply on the dangers of teenage sex play, which they called "petting." Such modern liberties, they feared, could lead to premarital intercourse and all its unhappy consequences, from pregnancy to permanent disgrace. Realistic measures, such as new scientific advances in birth control and the prevention and cure of venereal disease, were never mentioned—due only in part to the Comstock Law. It remained socially unacceptable to teach adolescents to deal with their sexuality in this practical way.

*So Youth May Know; New Viewpoints on Sex and Love* by Roy Ernest Dickerson, written in 1930, heralded this return to repression. The book opens with descriptions of growth freaks and the results of castration—hardly a comforting subject for adolescent sensibilities. The long and dreary first chapter takes up hormones, heredity, chromosomes, conception, and detailed embryology, with some very obscure and technical illustrations. This scientific veneer disappears in the second chapter, when Dickerson poses the question "Abstinence or promiscuity?" In case a youth should opt for the latter, he reminds readers that "drugstore" methods of birth control are only 60 percent effective and abortion is murder.

Dickerson's style is tedious and overwritten, and becomes even more labored when he takes up the subject of petting.

> At the very outset it must be said that it would be indeed ultra-puritanical and ill-advised to denounce altogether all the ordinary minor, more or less incidental, and chiefly matter-of-fact physical contacts between the sexes. . . . The first girl a boy thinks of for a "petting party" is not often the first one he thinks of for a wife. She may be all right for his "good times," but ordinarily he does not want "second-hand goods," or a woman who has been freely "pawed over" for sweetheart, wife, and

> mother of his children! . . . The boy who . . . thinks it is smart to "mess around" with girls, who—to be plain-spoken—has intercourse with first one and then another girl may very seriously affect his thinking and feeling about girls. He may never become able to be genuinely and permanently interested in any one girl.

To develop self-mastery over these unwelcome sexual temptations, Dickerson offers a collection of preventative techniques that come directly from Victorian antimasturbatory literature: keep busy; don't drink; pray; keep your bowels open; walk about rapidly; shadowbox; go through calisthenic exercises—and remember that kissing transmits syphilis.

Also in *So Youth May Know*, Dickerson broaches the forbidden subject of homosexuality: "A man who differs in this way is very unfortunate to say the least. . . . He is usually very uncomfortable and unhappy about it. . . . The medical specialists known as psychiatrists are often able to help a homosexual become quite normal." Women, on the other hand, do not have nearly as many sexual problems as men, according to Dickerson: "A woman's sexual energies are apt to be largely diverted into the maternal channel." Men should respect women's heroism in this, though, because "childbirth may involve suffering unequalled in masculine experience." This denial of feminine sexual enjoyment is reflected in the omission of the clitoris from the diagram of the female sex organs that appears as an appendix. Other subjects that are relegated to the appendixes are venereal disease, the male sexual anatomy, and masturbation (occasional incidents are acceptable, but habitual indulgence is not). Dickerson wrote another book in 1933, *Growing into Manhood*, which was more popularly written but expressed essentially the same ideas.

A widely respected title, and the last of the "bully boys" texts, was *In Training* (1933) by Thurman Brooks Rice, professor of bacteriology and pathology at the University of Indiana School of Medicine. The author's prestige and his hearty, outdoorsy approach made *In Training* the only sex education book to be recommended in the Boy Scout handbook for many years. The text is liberally decorated with photos of boys at sports, and the style is bluff and manly. "There isn't any doubt that the fellow who is strong and healthy has a big lead in these times when every one has to be on his toes," Rice begins. "The real man is a fighter" he points out, and holds up Teddy Roosevelt as a prime example of manliness. With this preamble, he launches into the familiar tale of sperm and ova and birth (which he terms "a considerable ordeal"). As to the father's role in fertilization, well, it resembles the relationship of the bee and the pollen but "the details are, of course, different." When intercourse is imminent (between married people) "the male penis becomes much larger and stiff." It is then moved in and out of the vagina; there is a pleasurable sensation; the muscles contract and inject sperm cells into the vagina. Rice explains that the purpose of intercourse is (1) children and (2) pleasure, and, although methods of preventing conception do exist, it is not fitting for a doctor to pass this knowledge on to inexperienced boys. Among the hazards of premature intercourse Rice emphasizes venereal disease, which causes death, blindness, and terrible deformity. There is a treatment for venereal disease but it is long, painful, expensive, and uncertain. Nevertheless, "I don't want you to be good because you are afraid to be otherwise," he reassures.

Further reassurance is offered about masturbation. The old stories are certainly untrue, but a boy who does it "too much" will be tired and weak, and "the fellow who sneaks off to a dark corner to practice masturbation is going to feel pretty badly about it." Athletics, Scouting, and hiking will help a boy keep his thoughts off sex. It also helps to use light bed covers, to go to bed tired, and to eschew "sissy" love stories.

Rice never mentions homosexuality by name, but he refers obliquely to "several other methods of sexual abuse, which are even more disgusting" than masturbation. "Persons who practice these methods are looked on with greatest contempt by all normal persons," and are "utterly ruined for all normal" sex. Nocturnal emissions and morning erections, however, are entirely normal. One should pay no attention to the scare literature of quacks or believe in the "wild oats" fallacy, which leads to venereal disease. Home and family are the cornerstone of society, and a boy should never do anything that would injure his future children.

In the same year (1933) Thurman Rice also wrote a companion volume for girls called *How Life Goes On and On; A Story for Girls of High School Age*. Here he is as enthusiastic in encouraging female passivity (in preparation for motherhood) as he had been in urging male aggressiveness through sports: "Domestic arts are of vast importance to the welfare of the human race." Teachers, as career women themselves, are prone to hold up before girls the ideal of a brilliant career, he observes. This is all right, but girls should remember that the family is most important and motherhood is the best career. Rice describes the function of the female reproductive organs (pregnancy) and the physiology of the male organs, although he omits the specific description of intercourse that he offered to boys. Sex "is perfectly proper when the man and woman are husband and wife" he assures his readers. Menstruation is not a sickness, although girls should avoid chilling and excess exercise during their periods. "Excess" exercise he defines as basketball, hockey, or swimming, adding that "Girls should not indulge in athletics that require long periods of training or excessive effort; they should go in for individual rather than for competitive effort." Vigorous sports train "blood vessels to favor the muscles rather than the organs of reproduction." Girls "must not permit improper relations" under penalty of venereal disease or pregnancy, and they are prettier if they don't drink or smoke. Rice deplores modern morality—"There are coming to be a number of people who think that marriage and the vows made in the wedding ceremony are old-fashioned and that they need not be observed"—and reiterates his theme: intelligent women should use their energies to bear children for the good of the race and not leave this important function to less bright housewives.

## Sex Education Books in the Library

How readily available were these books to teenagers? Until the 1930s the dissemination of sex information—whether by book, pamphlet, or word of mouth—had been seen as primarily the parents' job. Sex education books addressed to teenagers often added prefaces for parents assuring them that it was safe to "put this volume into the hands of your son or daughter." But in the course of this decade there were signs that many librarians were beginning to feel a responsibility for stocking and distributing sex information. This new idea caused considerable discomfort to older librarians, who had, after all, learned their own sexual attitudes from Stall and his peers. A controversy developed that still occasionally arises when two generations confront each other in the library profession.

During the thirties the *Wilson Library Bulletin* ran a monthly column in which readers were invited, each issue, to contribute their solutions to a specified library problem. The following month the replies to that question were printed, and cash prizes were awarded for the best solutions. The problem posed in the January 1934 issue came from an anxious librarian from a midwestern town who wrote:

> What should one do when a small boy, about fourteen years old, whose family I am not acquainted with but who seems of a quiet and rather studious temperament, comes into our public library and shyly asks for a book that will tell him "all about boys and girls and things like that"?

There is no school library here, and we do not have any "sex books" in our library of less than 11,000 volumes. I wonder if I did wrong in telling the boy that he would have to go to his parents for instruction in such matters. I do not know of any books of this nature that it would be safe to put into the hands of an adolescent, though I believe there are some especially written for the purpose. And, furthermore, it seems to me that many conservative parents would object to having the librarian interfere in this delicate phase of education. Just what are the librarian's duties in such a case, and what should be her course of procedure? I should very much appreciate hearing the opinion of others in your valuable publication.

There were twenty-six responses. The consensus was that the librarian was remiss in not providing the information, although many felt that it was advisable to stall for time in which to contact discreetly the parents for permission. A goodly number were of the opinion that supplying sex information was none of the library's business. Others suggested keeping the books locked up, circulating them only to young people who presented written permission from their parents. The more liberal letters indignantly stated that a library of 11,000 volumes definitely ought to have a few books on sex; some of these letters also pointed out that any boy who got up the courage to ask for such information at the library probably did so because he had been failed at home by tongue-tied parents.

The *Bulletin* itself, in an editorial comment, came out staunchly on the liberal side: "The librarian who interposes a barrier between the child and an essential part of his education is failing her duty to society, is weaving another strand into the net of taboos and inhibitions and circumlocutions that enmesh the adolescent and from which modern psychologists and educators would set him free." These brave stands were not backed with sound bibliographic knowledge, however, as is shown by the very few titles that were actually recommended in the letters. Several mentioned encyclopedias, adult physiology or genetics textbooks, or nature books for children. A few referred vaguely to pamphlets from the government or the American Social Hygiene Association. The two titles that were most frequently named were *Growing Up* by Karl De Schweinitz and *The Way Life Begins* by Bertha Cady. Four other titles rated one mention each: *The Sex Side of Life* by Mary Ware Dennett; *What Every Boy and Girl Should Know* by Margaret Sanger; *So Youth May Know* by Roy Dickerson; and Marie Stopes's much-banned *The Human Body*. The Self and Sex series, too, received its share of praise.

## The Late Thirties

A book that closely resembled those of De Schweinitz and Cady in its biological approach was *Being Born* (1936) by Frances Strain. The title is still in use with younger children, the third edition having been issued in 1970. The chapter headings show an organization that follows the pattern set by the two earlier authors: "Where the egg is made," "Where the sperm is made," "Two uniting cells," "From embryo to baby," "Coming into the world," "Like father, like son," "Mating and marrying." Strain adds a new dimension to her presentation of biological facts by including several questions from young people at the end of each topic, a method that allows her to raise psychological and ethical problems and to discuss teenagers' apprehensions without making these issues the focus of her book. As a literary technique, the question-and-answer format soon became a common feature of sex education books.

Strain's description of intercourse, while somewhat hushed and unearthly, is a bit more informative than De Schweinitz's:

> Outwardly the father and mother lie close together, arms about each other, while the sperm-bearing fluid enters into the mother by way of the perfectly fitting passages. . . . The sperm should be able to find the egg cell and fertilize it. It doesn't always, and if it doesn't, another mating must take place. . . . Because mating is also a way of expressing their love, husbands and wives unite when no baby is to be started. . . . Mating takes place in quiet and seclusion . . . the presence of another person would spoil the deep inner feelings.

The controversial subject of birth control is touched upon briefly and cautiously: "If a husband and wife decide they should not have children, then the sperm cell must not be allowed to enter the uterus and find the egg cell." For further clarification she explains "one may have a baby though one is not married" but unwed mothers "lead a sorry life."

A chapter on conception and embryology elicits the question "Does the mother have to tell the father when she is pregnant?" Strain describes birth from the baby's point of view. Labor pains, she asserts, are natural, but anesthetics can be given if the mother "becomes tired." The use of forceps is often helpful and is not harmful to the baby. A mother stays two weeks in the hospital afterwards. The questions on birth reveal young readers' anxiety: Does birth hurt a lot? What is a Caesarian?

The new science of genetics is the basis for a chapter on heredity, chromosomes, genetic defects, and birthmarks. Strain takes a stand against miscegenation: "Mixed marriages between races so widely different as Negroes and whites or as Chinese and whites are not thought to be desirable. The children suffer. They feel that they do not belong." On mating and marriage, she avoids the sentimental pitfalls of Growing Up, but copies that title in using statuary to illustrate the nude human body. She urges caution in choosing a marriage partner because "We must save the love acts and the mating acts for the chosen one." The book ends with a glossary of scientific terms, another innovation that was soon to become standard practice.

The pervading fear of sex outside of marriage was summed up in an extremely influential and widely reprinted article published by the Reader's Digest in August 1937—"The Case for Chastity" by Margaret Culkin Banning. Addressed only to young girls, the article was in preparation over a year. The author claimed to have spent that time interviewing doctors and psychologists about "the widespread whispering campaign that is now condoning unchastity and even advocating premarital relations." In her research she discovered that 5 percent of Americans had syphilis and 10 percent gonorrhea. Banning also came to the conclusion that contraceptives are only partially effective, and she quotes Hannah Stone, the director of the birth control clinic founded by Margaret Sanger, to this effect: vaginal jelly is only 60 percent safe, suppositories 40 to 50 percent safe, and douches only 10 percent. (She does not include any statistics on the condom and diaphragm, long known to be the most effective forms of birth control.) The dangers of abortion are also well known, Banning reminds readers. In spite of all this modern talk, she says, men still prefer virgins for wives. Clandestine sex is uncomfortable, and the girl is usually abandoned afterward and may become promiscuous. Banning points out that girls naturally have a sense of guilt about illicit sex even if they are not religious. If the couple eventually marry, their earlier experience may give them cause not to trust each other later. Nor is petting a safe substitute—it may unfit a woman for satisfaction in "normal sex relations." Banning recommends early marriage as a solution, with financial help from the parents if necessary. The article exactly summed up popular attitudes, if not practices, and continued to be recommended in bibliographies. As late as 1962 it was reprinted in the Reader's Digest, substantially cut, but with its message essentially unchanged.

Two books that were far above the rest of the genre at this time in presenting humane and sensible sex advice were Attaining Manhood; A Doctor Talks to Boys about Sex (1938) and Attaining Wom-

*anhood; A Doctor Talks to Girls about Sex* (1939) by George Washington Corner. The author, a professor of anatomy at the University of Rochester,* writes in a simple, direct, and friendly style and conveys more information in sixty-seven pages than most of the far wordier books that appeared in the next two decades. He presents the anatomical facts with spare precision, and within the context of the sex attitudes of the thirties, he is calmly matter-of-fact about sex behaviors. The anatomical drawings, although not done by Corner himself, are remarkable for their clarity.

*Attaining Manhood* is addressed to "the intelligent boy of high school age." Corner catches that reader's attention immediately by admitting in his first sentence that "everybody is interested in sex." But why has nature arranged things in this way? So that every living creature has more than one single line of ancestry, he explains. A clear description of the function of the sperm and ova in fish, birds, and mammals follows. In the next chapter, on the human reproductive system, Corner the anatomist is at his best. With the sureness of the man who knows his subject, he describes the structure and function of the male and female reproductive systems, using correct technical terms and illustrating the text with crystal-clear drawings. "Some practical matters" are dealt with in an aside printed in a different typeface—worries about undescended testicles, varicoceles, and penis size.

When it comes to describing the central event of sex, however, Corner shies away: "In the act of mating the sperm cells are deposited in the vagina." He justifies his approach by explaining that "Sex attraction in the human race is not a subject which can be dealt with on a purely scientific basis." Furthermore, "About human sex desire the important thing to remember is that it depends upon attraction of the mind as well as the body." However, the physical changes in puberty can be described scientifically, and Corner does so, using a simple nude drawing to illustrate. He points out that in primitive societies manhood was acknowledged at an early age through puberty rites, whereas in modern society, physical maturity precedes marriage by several years.

Corner now offers comfort on the two traditionally worrisome topics of nocturnal emissions and masturbation. The former is "thought by some scientists to have a useful purpose, being perhaps

*Corner was evidently an exceptional teacher; at least two of his former students remember his classes as being instrumental in inspiring their outstanding careers in sex education: William Howell Masters, author of *Human Sexual Response*, and Alan Guttmacher, who served as president of the Planned Parenthood Federation.

a method by which old stale sperm cells are cleared out in order to make room for a fresh supply from the testes." No sensible boy should pay any attention to the "wicked nonsense" of quacks on the subject. Masturbation is something that "all boys discover for themselves," and it "happens at one time or another to practically every boy and man." Although it is admittedly unnatural and secretive, masturbation is not the terrible thing it has been made out to be. People who offer advice with "an air of horror" have often caused "tragic mental suffering." Corner himself would explain the practice as a kind of substitute for intercourse, because, as he has explained, marriage is ordinarily postponed in our society. However, he is quick to add a counterargument: "People who expect to do well in study and on the playing field cannot permit themselves to yield to every mood of self-indulgence. . . . Sensible boys and men will avoid as far as possible unnecessary sexual stimulations, especially those which tend to cheapen and degrade one's ideas of sex."

"In girls the sex feelings are not expressed in quite the same way as in boys," Corner continues. "Girls," he says, "tend to have much vaguer sex thoughts and feelings. Whether a girl knows much or little about the facts of sex and reproduction, her own emotions are not at first directed toward actual physical sex actions. In fact the thought of sexual relations is often distasteful. Usually it is only when completely under the sway of love that frank sexual desires are developed." Introducing male readers to menstruation, Corner emphasizes the mystery of the process rather than its known purposes: "For reasons which are still very puzzling to science, females of the human race (and also some of the higher animals) are subject to periodic bleeding from the uterus." He gives no further explanation of the function of the menses, but does caution boys that girls' cycles are responsible for changes of mood and disposition.

As presented in *Attaining Manhood*, the problem of human sex conduct is how to behave as an animal with a mind. Corner sees some rules as just good biology—the incest taboo, for instance. Other rules are universal throughout humanity: "The human race has decided . . . that the ideal expression of sex is the life-long union of marriage." Any other sexual relationship can be considered immoral, he states flatly. There are many temptations to break this rule, but boys should remember that prostitutes transmit venereal disease and satisfy the animal nature only. Petting or necking is "playing with dynamite" and may result in pregnancy and "grave embarrassment and difficulty." The only safe course is to say "no to all physical intimacies" outside of marriage.

The final chapter of *Attaining Manhood*, on sex disorders, provides a brief and factual description of the symptoms of syphilis and gonorrhea, and warns boys that not only prostitutes may be carriers, but also "any persons who may be willing to take part in illicit sexual relations." Protection is "dangerously uncertain," and while Corner freely admits that venereal disease is curable, he adds that the treatment is long and painful. A second class of sex disorder is homosexuality, which Corner discusses much more freely than earlier writers, most of whom found the subject too distasteful to mention. He says, "Strange as it may seem, there are a few men who develop sexual attraction toward members of their own sex; a man so disturbed is interested only in sexual contacts with other men and boys. This quirk of the mind is called 'homosexuality.' . . . To normal men it is a very disgusting thing, but the person involved is not to be considered wicked but rather as the victim of a disease. Skillful treatment by a physician experienced in mental guidance may in fact cure the aberration." Corner confuses homosexuals with child molesters, a misunderstanding that was to be nearly universal among sex educators for the next twenty years. A boy who is approached by one of these unfortunate men, he counsels, should seek out the advice of an older man he trusts.

In *Attaining Womanhood* (1939) girls are given almost the same anatomical instruction as the boys, with one interesting difference— Corner seems to have become aware of the function of the sex hormones estrogen and progesterone sometime between the writing of the two books. He mentions them several times, and in the description of menstruation, a phenomenon that in the earlier book he found "still puzzling to science," he gives a full account of their function as triggering mechanisms. Another ground-breaking inclusion in this title is a complete drawing of the female *external* genitalia with all the parts labeled, including the clitoris.

As might be expected, *Attaining Womanhood* has far more detailed information about pregnancy and birth than the boy's book. There are diagrams of the relative size and position of the growing "child" in the uterus, and a description of the birth process that, to some extent, acknowledges the woman's role as an active one: "With modern anesthetics and skilled medical help the discomforts of childbirth are lightened." Corner discredits the old wives' tale that a woman can transfer a "maternal impression" or physical mark to her unborn baby if she experiences any severe shock or trauma during pregnancy.

Corner advises girls on the differences in sexual attitudes between men and women: "A man's part in sex life and reproduction is only a small part of his activity; the woman's part requires much of her life." Women want love and devotion, but with men and mature boys sex thoughts are "more frank and outspoken." Their urges are "more physical, less vague, and more easily aroused than a girl's." In a passage that foreshadows the sexism that was to be a prominent part of sex education in the fifties, Corner counsels girls on choosing a husband: "In the case of a woman who marries, the general rule that a woman's work is done through other people is intensified. In selecting a mate she is choosing the workshop in which she is to do her life's work, selecting the instruments with which to make her mark in the world."

Under "Sex Problems" for girls, Corner lists the anxiety of achieving personal attractiveness, self-excitement (masturbation), and crushes. The latter, consisting of passionate attachments between girls "verging on the sexual," "may cause difficulty in making proper adjustments to the other sex." But he does not class crushes with homosexuality, which "may be an inborn trait, a deformity of the instincts; in other cases it is believed to be set up as a result of unfortunate circumstances in youth." Homosexuals can be cured, he maintains. "Many homosexual women, are, moreover, able to control this tendency and turn their energies into useful service," he says. Such tendencies "may be acquired by association," so a girl should take care to avoid a woman who makes physical advances. Other sexual annoyances for young girls are exhibitionists and men who touch or fondle girls in crowds. Neither are dangerous, only pitiful and unpleasant for the girl.

One of many pamphlets printed by the YMCA was The Other Sex (1939) by Dora Hudson Klemer, a "physician, social worker and mother." Imparting the then conventional advice about sexual physiology and hygiene, Klemer follows Corner's lead in including a glossary and a diagram of both male and female external genitalia. The pamphlet is characteristic of the time in its emphasis on the need for maintaining chastity, a condition that Klemer defines as "a clean slate, with nothing to unlearn." She enumerates drawbacks to unchastity in two lists, one for each sex. For girls there is the fear of pregnancy (because no birth control used outside marriage and without the clinical advice of a doctor is safe); the dangers of abortion; guilt, which spoils the thrill of marriage; and the fact that boys don't marry unchaste girls. The list for boys points out that sex is not necessary for health; prostitutes have venereal disease; and there is risk of pregnancy for the girl. Above all, promiscuous young men have unhappy marriages, and never experience the supreme expression of love or learn the discipline of self-control, which is necessary in all areas of life.

Several relics of the past were issued in new editions at the end of the decade. In 1936 the Self and Sex series was reprinted (for the last time) almost unchanged from its revision ten years earlier. Irving Steinhardt's *Ten Sex Talks to Girls* and *Ten Sex Talks to Boys*, first printed in 1914, were reissued as *Sex Talks to Girls* and *Sex Talks to Boys* in 1938 and 1940, respectively. The advice to young men is very little updated—boys are still warned of the dangers of the public toilet and assured that "venereal diseases are well-nigh incurable" and that masturbation produces insanity. They are urged to dissuade girls from immodest dress and paint, and to check their sisters' wardrobes frequently to make sure that they are not being given extravagant gifts by ill-intentioned men.

As Steinhardt explains in the preface, *Sex Talks to Girls* also has few changes from the first edition "because decency and right living and the ways of avoiding diseases of the sexual tract do not change." His book, he brags, "has outlived the lurid, exciting, arousing and vicious books on this subject because it was clean but instructive." In a gesture toward modernity, he does include a diagram of the female external genitalia in which the clitoris appears but is not labeled. However, he still maintains that the hymen is rarely destroyed in any other way but by an attempt to introduce something into the vagina, and advises girls that a signed statement should be secured from a doctor if it is necessary to interfere with the hymen. The ghastly photo of a syphilitic baby remains, as does his plea to girls to "endeavor to bring back to the 'straight and happy path' of virtue those girls who have strayed from it."

Steinhardt continues to attack the corset as a "fashionable" contraption (in 1939) and further scolds young girls for sporting immodest modern dress: "If a man came up to you in the street and, without speaking to you, merely reached down and raised your skirts in order to see your lower limbs, you would think him insane, or grossly insulting. Yet that is what your present mode of dressing would suggest that you wanted, except that you freely expose yourself to view without giving any man the trouble of having to lift your clothing." Other targets of his wrath are "paint," "dances whose poses or steps are suggestive," drinking, flirting ("You cannot act like a 'fallen' woman and not expect to be treated as such"), accepting rides from strangers, meeting men on street corners, and "pick-ups."

## Institutional Books of the Forties

As World War II approached, sex education became a minor issue indeed. Young men in their late teens, sent off to war and the possibility of an early death, abandoned traditional sexual codes as meaningless. These lapses society found excusable, if not totally acceptable, but the seeds of change had been sown.

For these reasons, and because shortages of paper curtailed civilian printing, there were very few sex education books printed during the war years. Those that did appear were sponsored by schools or churches, and were meant to be used in those institutions. The one exception is *Love at the Threshold* (1942) by Frances Strain (author of *Being Born*), a book that was addressed to college-age young people and emphasized conventional morality in a setting of romantic love and early marriage—but without mentioning the war in any way. There was a large gap between the advice of Strain and other older sex educators and the advice handed out by the U.S. Army with free condoms—"If you can't be good, be careful!"

*A Boy Grows Up* (1940) by Harry C. McKown is an example of the institutional "teen life" book of the forties. The author, editor of *School Activities*, writes in a pompous and didactic style but adopts a phony veneer of teen slang. The book is typical of those designed for supplementary reading in social hygiene courses called "Senior Problems" or "Life Adjustment." There are many, many chapters on problems of gaining social maturity—managing finances, education, recreation, etiquette, friendships, nutrition, health, alcohol, and tobacco—and one chapter on sex, which is largely devoted to discouraging masturbation. "Even though, if practiced moderately, masturbation does not cause insanity or disease, it is hardly advisable . . ." because it is "done secretly and is, therefore, generally accompanied by a feeling of wrong-doing." In the time-honored manner, McKown gives a list of twelve ways to avoid not only masturbation but even erections: keep the bowels clear, have a hobby, exercise self-control, change position frequently when seated, and so on.

The controversy among librarians as to their responsibilities in sex education had become heated by 1941. In that year Frances Strain was invited to be the featured speaker at the Illinois Library

Association's annual conference. She told the assembled librarians that the circulation of sex education books should not be restricted except in the case of definitely technical works. She also urged the profession to develop a better understanding of sex education and to have in mind some reliable suggestions to offer parents and teachers—presumably including *Being Born* and *Love at the Threshold*.

An example of the pamphlet meant to be used by biology teachers in a unit on reproduction is *Life Goes On* (1942) by Jessie Williams Clemensen and others. (A trio of educators collaborated in producing the pamphlet's thirty-five pages—Clemenson and Freda Buckingham Daniels, both high school teachers, and William Ralph La Porte, professor of physical education and chairman of the division of health and physical education at the University of Southern California.) The authors proposed to counsel the young facing the puzzling question "How can I maintain a wholesome relationship with the opposite sex?" The answer, couched in dry and stuffy prose, has much to say about mitosis and Mendel's law, but very little about making love. (A chart of the male sex organs, with Victorian reticence, ignores the penis.) Inspirational quotes head each chapter (" 'Sex is never low and unworthy unless it is made so by a low and unworthy person'—Dr. Florence Meredith"). A section on venereal disease states that syphilis is now curable if treated early, and that gonorrhea is spread mostly by intercourse and almost never by door knobs, food, towels, or toilet seats. However, the authors remind boys that 90 percent of prostitutes have gonorrhea.

A discussion of the stages of personality growth leads to the subject of petting (under "Special Problems"). This practice the authors describe as "a selfish experiment in sexual sensation by two people who have little true interest in the future welfare of each other." There are serious dangers in petting: (1) The possibility of contracting syphilis or other diseases spread by kissing, (2) overstimulation of the ductless glands, (3) acquisition of a reputation as a "petter" or "necker," and (4) loss of control. The intimate sex relations that may follow loss of control "nearly always" have tragic results, including one or more of the following: serious psychological conditions caused by fear, distrust, jealousy, shame, remorse, or loss of self-respect; blocked emotional maturity; infection with venereal disease; forced marriage; illegitimate children; illegal abortions, which often cause death or invalidism; decreased chances for marriage; and decreased chances for happiness in marriage. How, then, to control the sex instinct? The authors suggest yet another list: (1) stay in groups, (2) avoid suggestive books, magazines, and movies,

(3) avoid vulgar conversation, (4) keep the mind occupied with wholesome things like school, church, home duties, and hobbies, (5) exercise, (6) avoid alcohol, and (7) follow one's best impulses.

Around this time a few churches also began to prepare sex education pamphlets for use in Christian education classes. A fairly conservative example is Alice M. Hustad's *Strictly Confidential for Young Girls*, published in 1944 in Minnesota by the Board of Parish Education. Speaking from a "background of Christian philosophy," Hustad takes on such topics of interest to teenage girls as personality, grooming, and mental health through Christianity. She wastes no time equivocating on questions such as how to prevent venereal disease—just don't have sex before marriage: "God promised punishment to those who abuse the sex life by sinful, impure desires of lust" so those who contract venereal disease get what they deserve. Questions and answers on dating focus on the hazards of blind dates, going steady, dutch treats, drinking, and smoking.

Hustad disapproves of the ballroom: "Since dancing removes many barriers to intimacy, a girl may be easily led to permit intimacies which she will later regret." Girls are forearmed to resist these intimacies if they are aware of the arguments a boy may use "to convince a girl to gratify his sex 'desires.' " He might call her old-fashioned, break down her resistance with petting and alcohol, tell her nobody will know, assure her of his love, ask her to prove their compatibility, and accuse her of frigidity. Nor is there safety in contraceptives—they "fail repeatedly." Girls should also beware of "homo-sexualists": "If any girl wants you to be her friend alone, and if she insists upon 'cuddling' or other physical contacts, avoid her entirely." Madame Chiang Kai-shek is held up as a shining example of womanhood. Wise girls will emulate her, and use the teen years to prepare for marriage responsibilities. The ideal girl will "study the art of pleasing a husband and learn to taste of the sweetness of humility and submission"—a theme that was soon to become the basis for the next phase of repressive sex education literature in the fifties.

## BIBLIOGRAPHY

Banning, Margaret Culkin. "The Case for Chastity." *Reader's Digest*, August 1937. Reprinted July 1962.

Cady, Bertha Louise Chapman. *The Way Life Begins; An Introduction to Sex Education*. New York: American Social Hygiene Association, 1917; rev. ed., 1939.

Clemensen, Jessie Williams et al. *Life Goes On*. New York: Harcourt, 1942.

Corner, George Washington. *Attaining Manhood; A Doctor Talks to Boys about Sex*. New York: Harper, 1938.

———. *Attaining Womanhood; A Doctor Talks to Girls about Sex*. New York: Harper, 1939.

De Schweinitz, Karl. *Growing Up: The Story of How We Become Alive, Are Born and Grow Up*. New York: Macmillan, 1928; 2nd rev. ed., 1945.

Dickerson, Roy Ernest. *Growing into Manhood*. New York: Association Press, 1933.

———. *So Youth May Know; New Viewpoints on Sex and Love*. New York: Association Press, 1930; rev ed., 1948.

Drake, Emma Frances Angell. *What a Woman of Forty-five Ought to Know*. Self and Sex Series. Philadelphia: Vir Publishing Co., 1928.

———. *What a Young Wife Ought to Know*. Self and Sex Series. Philadelphia: Vir Publishing Co., 1928; rev ed., 1936.

Hustad, Alice M. *Strictly Confidential for Young Girls*. Minneapolis, MN: Board of Parish Education, 1944.

Klemer, Dora Hudson. *The Other Sex: A Frank Statement, Addressed to Both Boys and Girls, of the Essential Facts that Young People Want and Need to Know about Sex*. New York: Association Press, 1939.

Lamson, Armenouhie Tashjian. *How I Came to Be (My Birth)*, 2nd ed., rev. and enl. New York: Macmillan, 1926.

Lindsey, Benjamin Barr. *Companionate Marriage*. Garden City, NY: Garden City Publishing Co., 1929.

———, and Evans, Wainwright. *The Revolt of Modern Youth*. New York: Boni and Liveright, 1925.

McKown, Harry C. *A Boy Grows Up*. New York: McGraw-Hill, 1940; 2nd ed., 1949.

Moore, Harry Hascall. *Keeping in Condition: A Handbook on Training for Older Boys*, rev. ed. New York: Macmillan, 1924.

Rice, Thurman Brooks. *How Life Goes On and On; A Story for Girls of High School Age*. Chicago: American Medical Association, 1933.

———. *In Training; For Boys of High School Age*. Chicago: American Medical Association, 1933.

Sanger, Margaret. *What Every Boy and Girl Should Know*. New York: Brentano's, 1927.

Spaller, Louise Frances. *Personal Help for Boys*. Marietta, OH: Mullikin, 1921.

———. *Personal Help for Girls*. Marietta, OH: Mullikin, 1918.

Stall, Sylvanus. *What a Man of Forty-five Ought to Know*. Self and Sex Series. Philadelphia: Vir Publishing Co., 1928.

———. *What a Young Boy Ought to Know*. Self and Sex Series. Philadelphia: Vir Publishing Co., 1926; rev. eds., 1928, 1936.

———. *What a Young Husband Ought to Know*. Self and Sex Series. Philadelphia: Vir Publishing Co., 1928; rev. ed., 1936.

———. *What a Young Man Ought to Know*. Self and Sex Series. Philadelphia: Vir Publishing Co., 1928; rev. ed., 1936.

Steinhardt, Irving David. *Sex Talks to Boys*, rev. ed. Philadelphia: Lippincott, 1940.

———. *Sex Talk to Girls (Twelve Years and Older)*, rev. ed. Philadelphia: Lippincott, 1938.

Stopes, Marie Carmichael. *Sex and the Young*. New York: Putnam, 1926.

Strain, Frances Bruce. *Being Born*. New York: Appleton-Century, 1936.

———. *Love at the Threshold*. New York: Appleton-Century-Crofts, 1942.

Swabacker, Leslie J. *Letters to My Daughter*. Chicago: Atwood and Knight, 1926.

"What to Do with the Youngster Who Asks for a Book of Sex-Information?" *Wilson Library Bulletin*. 8 (January 1934): 276–286.

Wood-Allen, Mary. *What a Young Girl Ought to Know*. Self and Sex Series. Philadelphia: Vir Publishing Co., 1928.

———. *What a Young Woman Ought to Know*. Self and Sex Series. Philadelphia: Vir Publishing Co., 1928; rev. ed., 1936.

# 6

# *The Dating Manuals*

After the agonies and uncertainties of World War II, America turned with relief to the stability of home and marriage and social conformity. In the literature of the period, male and female role behavior and relationships between the sexes became rigidly defined and were subject to prescribed expectations. During the war many women had taken on such jobs as welding and truck driving and had learned to make decisions for themselves. Now that the men were back home, it was necessary to return all the players to their accustomed places on the board so that the game of life could proceed as before.

Teenagers, with their natural desire for conformity, were especially vulnerable to these pressures. Boy-girl interaction was codified into the intricate ritual known as dating, and every adolescent was expected to participate. The rules were complex and exact, and covered every possible variation. In 1950 Evelyn Duvall, the leading authority on dating, laid out the basic pattern in *Facts of Life and Love for Teenagers*:

> John calls for Mary at her home at the appointed time. Mary is ready for John and answers the door herself when he rings (he has come to see her, not some other member of her family). She greets him pleasantly and leads him into the living room where her parents are waiting to meet him.
>
> Mary introduces John to her parents by saying something like this: "Mother, this is John. Dad, you remember John plays center on the team." This little lead as a part of the introduction gives Dad and John something to talk about at once. Dad may ask a simple question on how the team is going this season. John is put at his ease and answers, while Mother and Dad relax and enjoy getting acquainted with him.
>
> In a few moments Mary picks up her coat and, smiling at John, indicates that they had probably better be on their way. If John holds the

coat for Mary, she accepts his assistance graciously; if he does not, she slips into her coat without comment and prepares for departure.

As the couple is about to leave, Mary turns to her parents and says, "We are going to the Bijou for the double feature (or whatever), you know. We should be home before midnight (or whatever hour seems reasonable)." This declaration of plans and specifying of time for homecoming has a double purpose. It lets her folks know that she is taking responsibility for getting in before it is too late, and prevents them from putting down the parental foot too hard. Further, such initiative on Mary's part lets John know what is expected of him in getting Mary home. If Mary has already talked over their plans with her parents before John has arrived, her last-minute announcement is simply a confirmation for all four of them.

The couple leave, with John opening the door for Mary, while she accepts the courtesy with a smile. When they reach the box office, Mary steps back and looks at the display cards while John buys the tickets. Inside, if there is an usher, Mary follows him while John follows her down the aisle. If there is no usher on duty, John goes ahead and finds seats while Mary follows. Once seated, John helps Mary slip out of her coat and get settled. They enjoy the show without annoying their neighbors with talking, giggling, or other disturbing behavior.

Out of the theater, John may suggest something to eat or he may conduct Mary to the place of his choice. When he asks her what she would like to have, she thoughtfully hesitates until she sees what price range he has in mind. She says something like this: "What is good here, John?" or "What do you suggest?" If John recommends the steak sandwich with French fries, or the double-gooey sundae with nuts, this gives Mary the general idea of what he is prepared to spend. If she is friendly and shrewd she may note that John, in his desire to do the right thing, is suggesting something extravagant. If so, she will ask for something that she knows costs a little less. But if John says, "Which do you like better, coke or root beer?" Mary graciously keeps within these bounds. Over their food, John and Mary talk about the movie they have just seen or friends they have in common or anything that is of mutual interest. As they leave the restaurant, John pays the check and Mary thanks him by saying simply, "That was good; thank you, John."

Once back at Mary's house, Mary gets out her key, unlocks the door, and then turns to John with a smile. She says, "It's been a lovely evening. Thank you, John," or something similar that lets John know she has enjoyed the date. John replies, "I have enjoyed it, too. I'll be seeing you." Then she opens the door and goes in without further hesitation. Since this is the first date, neither John nor Mary expect a goodnight kiss. So Mary is careful not to linger at the door, which might make John wonder what she expects him to do.

Two purposes lie behind these elaborate social instructions. One is to limit the possibility of any expression of physical sexuality in a situation that is inherently sexual. The other is to train the girl to defer to and bolster the male ego at every turn. Thus society began to remind girls of their traditional feminine roles and to encourage them to put aside the new freedoms and responsibilities they had assumed while the men were away at war. That the pattern of early dating led to early marriage and the conventional integration of young men and women into society was the expected, and desired end. To ensure this outcome, however, it was necessary to prevent the couple from finding satisfaction within the dating pattern, so that their sexual tensions moved them inexorably toward a wedding.

Evelyn Duvall was the leading exponent of this intricately plotted dating ritual. Her *Facts of Life and Love for Teenagers* (1950, 1956, 1963) dominated the fifties in teen sex education, and in its latest edition continues to appear on conservative reading lists. It is the book that many women now in their forties—the age group that has provided most of the leadership of the women's movement—read and revered in their teens. Duvall was an eminently respectable doctor of sociology (although she was usually referred to as Mrs. Duvall). Very early in her career she began to specialize in marriage and the family—her doctoral thesis was entitled "Conceptions of Parenthood"—and was executive director of the Association for Family Living and subsequently executive secretary of the National Council on Family Relations. She lectured and taught widely, and for many years her voice was ubiquitous not only in the professional journals but also in popular magazines such as *Coronet, Reader's Digest*, and *Parents' Magazine.* Her picture in the 1947 issue of *Current Biography* shows a slim, pleasant-faced woman, impeccably groomed and coiffed and wearing a ladylike string of pearls at the neck of her tailored suit.

Duvall was a prolific writer. In addition to the three editions of *Facts of Life and Love for Teenagers*, she addressed young people's sexual problems in *When You Marry* (1945), *The Art of Dating* (1958, 1967), *Why Wait Till Marriage?* (1965), and numerous pamphlets and articles. For children she wrote *About Sex and Growing Up* (1968), and for parents, *Today's Teen-agers* (1966). With her husband, a college professor (the Dr. Duvall) whom she had married immediately upon graduating from Syracuse University, she coauthored two books: *Sense and Nonsense about Sex* (1962) and *Sex Ways—In Fact and Faith* (1961). He alone wrote *101 Questions to Ask Yourself before You Marry* (1950), which was changed to *Before*

*You Marry* in the 1959 edition. But it was *Facts of Life and Love* that remained the classic for teenagers in the fifties. Because it was the model for middle-class teen behavior for an entire generation, and because the other sex education books of that period echo its dictates point for point, it is worth looking at in some detail.

## Duvall and the Dating Ritual

Not since *What a Young Boy Ought to Know* had there been a teen sex education book that so exactly caught the mood of its times. Duvall's advanced degrees won her the trust of the fifties establishment, just as Stall's clerical background had done in his time. Both authors agreed on the essential message: sex is extremely dangerous unless rigorously controlled. Duvall compares it to electricity, which, when harnessed, can light homes, cook meals, and warm feet, but when left to run wild as lightning, can "hurt and destroy and leave forever scarred all that you hold dear."

Duvall's writing is thoughtful and moderate, sprightly but not cute. "Lively" is the word that was most often applied by her contemporaries. Her work shows serious research (although her bias sometimes keeps her from completely assimilating new facts), but the tone is always human and warm. Perhaps Duvall's most serious limitation, other than the rigid concept of correct male/female behavior imposed by her times, is a certain naive lack of humor. However, her dignity and good sense save her from attempts at teen slang—a mistake that made some other books quickly out-of-date and ridiculous.

The first two chapters of *Facts of Life and Love*, one for boys and one for girls, go over the physical facts of puberty and internal reproductive anatomy. Girls are advised on menstruation, bras and girdles, and skin problems, and boys are told that, although "our grandfathers feared that the loss of semen somehow meant the loss of manhood," wet dreams are no cause for alarm, nor is it necessary to have intercourse to develop normally. A new interest in "grown-up matters" for girls is equated with "relationships with boys, hairdos, fashions, and love stories." This implied narrowness of female interests is emphasized in a paragraph on "Learning to be a woman." According to Duvall, femininity means learning to love and be loved, to enjoy boys and men as persons, and to enjoy the fine arts of being a real woman. Masculinity, by contrast, involves learning to establish oneself with other boys and men as an accepted member of

the male community, learning to love girls, attaining secure economic and social status as an adult male, and searching for the meaning
of life and the answer to the question "Who am I?"

In the next chapter Duvall takes up the more easily answered
question "Where do babies come from?" This information, she feels,
was formerly hard to find: "Books may be written on the subject, but
often the library does not have them, or they are kept out of sight in
conformity with the taboo that still exists in some places against
reading or discussing such things." Duvall remedies the apparent
lack with a brief description of pregnancy, birth, and heredity. The
illustrations in this section are photographs of an exhibit on human
reproduction from the Museum of Science and Industry in Chicago.
Although earnest in attempting to depict these processes accurately,
they are not entirely successful; they lack contrast and the print is
too small for easy reading. The photographs seem especially cumbersome in comparison to the bouncy little sketches from teen life that
illustrate the rest of the book. Drawn by Ruth Belew, these cartoons
make up for Duvall's lack of humor; they were widely imitated, and
probably had a great deal to do with the book's success.

Duvall turns next to the problems that can come from the misuse
of sexuality. The first of "Sex troubles and worries" ("Sex problems
and promises" in the 1956 edition) is "getting into trouble," that is,
illicit pregnancy. In the 1956 edition she quotes a study by Leontyne
Young that showed that many girls deliberately allow themselves to
get pregnant in order to get back at parents, or in imitation of a promiscuous mother or sister, or because they are starved for affection.
Other girls, says Duvall, may be the victims of older men, or have sex
on impulse, or lack knowledge of the workings of their bodies. Once
a girl has conceived, she will have to go through with the pregnancy
because abortion is illegal and dangerous and is considered immoral
by many religious groups. However, her parents and social welfare
agencies can help her. Regarding contraception, Duvall admits that
"several methods work satisfactorily when prescribed by a competent physician," but she doesn't recommend or describe any of
them and notes that preventing conception is not only a personal
issue but a social question—the Catholic Church, for instance, considers it a mortal sin.

Other "Sex troubles and worries" are prostitution, venereal disease, homosexuality, and masturbation. The first she condemns for
social rather than moral reasons: "Not only is it bad in itself, in that
it capitalizes on the exploitative impulses of man and enslaves woman, but it also is a basic factor in civic corruption and a common

breeding place for venereal disease." The symptoms of syphilis and gonorrhea are briefly described; both can be cured by early diagnosis and care, she admits, but the "only sure protection is in restricting sexual intercourse to marriage."

Published in 1948, Alfred Kinsey's *Sexual Behavior in the Human Male* had appeared two years before the first edition of *Facts of Life and Love for Teenagers.* Duvall was too good a social scientist to pretend she was not aware of Kinsey's finding that at least one-third of American men had had a homosexual experience at some time in their lives, but in her writing for teenagers she displayed a cautionary ambivalence about this topic. Kinsey's influence is evident in Duvall's admission in *Facts of Life and Love* that "most people at some time in their lives have experienced some kind of homosexual tie" and in her explanation of sexual behavior as a continuum, or scale, from homosexuality to heterosexuality: "At the homosexual end of the scale are persons whose sexual interests involve members of the same sex exclusively; at the other end of the scale are men and women who are interested in members of the other sex only; in between is the large number of persons of both sexes who at some time in their lives and to some extent find their own sex appealing, but whose capacities for responding to the other sex are also well developed."

Like many teen sex educators who wrote in the years immediately following the release of Kinsey's findings, however, Duvall still saw homosexuality as a disease—"Sometimes our earliest experiences with people give us little faith in them or in ourselves or in love itself, and so we may develop twisted feelings about others and distorted ways of responding to them"—and a menace—"The boy who has been approached by an older man in ways that do not seem quite right to him should avoid further opportunities to be alone with this particular individual. Sound counseling help is also needed by the boy who has been inducted into homosexual activities and has become deeply involved emotionally." Her conclusion is that "we" should get over our anxieties about it, and "understand it as a not unusual part of growing up, although its overt forms are not to be actively sought."

Masturbation can be another anxiety-causing subject. "Not long ago," she reminds boys, people thought masturbation caused insanity, and some persons still think it is a sin. Others believe it can be detected by circles under the eyes, pimples, or a peculiar look in the eye. All nonsense, she maintains stoutly, "Today we know that the tendency to relieve sexual tension by rubbing the genital area to the point of release is a very common practice. Statistical studies and clinical findings indicate that between 80 and 90 percent of teen-age boys report that they masturbate, and that somewhat fewer teen-age girls also report the practice." However, masturbation can exaggerate a tendency to be withdrawn and solitary, and "some authorities report that a history of masturbation on the part of the woman, and in some cases of men too, makes more difficult the adjustments to the marriage partner later. Some girls who have stimulated themselves to the point of release for years before marriage may require exactly the same type of frictional excitation from their husbands after marriage in order to achieve full release from sexual tension." In the final analysis, Duvall decides that "one finds it hard to say that masturbation, therefore, is right or wrong, harmless or harmful; it all depends upon the many interrelated factors in the individual involved."

The main body of *Facts of Life and Love*, however, is devoted to the minutiae of the dating ritual. Duvall has no doubts that every teenager will and should date, and offers no comfort to those who do not. Indeed, she makes it plain that she considers such failure to participate as willful, and demolishes excuses in a paragraph headed "If I only had. . . ." She advises that if things are a bit slow in getting started, girls may have to (subtly) take the initiative at first, because boys mature more slowly. The novice dater can expect to feel awkward but expertise soon develops—"You learn how to do it by doing it. At first you will feel somewhat uncomfortable in new situations and embarrassed in unexpected predicaments. But with experience you polish off the rough edges and become smooth."

Duvall explores correct dating technique in all its aspects: telephone etiquette, accepting and giving gifts, how to ask a girl out (never say, "What are you doing Friday night?"), last minute invitations, accepting a date graciously, being stood up, what to do and where to go on a date, conversation on a date, costs, responding to a "line," introductions, being friendly to a date's grandparents, brothers, and sisters, what to wear ("stockings or socks, long dress or short, dress or skirt and sweater . . ."), hogging the bathroom when preparing for a date, borrowing clothes from other members of the family, deciding how late is all right, using the family car, and blind dates and double dates. Most parents "would prefer that their young people date those with the same general background—national, religious, social—as their own," she explains, and hints delicately at interracial dating problems: "Issues of tolerance, democracy, brotherhood, and fair play may seem more important to you than conforming to some tradition." Throughout, Duvall upholds the importance of conformity, as in her careful advice on the thin-ice situation of ridding oneself of a bad reputation or dating a serviceman.

Although the problem of "that goodnight kiss" can be a matter of regional custom, according to Duvall the general agreement is that the first date is too soon. But for necking and petting, never is too soon. The former she defines as "any love-making above the neck" and the latter as "the caressing of other more sensitive parts of the body in a crescendo of sexual stimulation." Petting is habit forming, she warns, because "these forces are often very strong and insistent. Once released, they tend to press for completion." To help daters know exactly when to apply the brakes, she provides a list of danger signs: the boy will react first, with flushed face, rapid breathing, pounding heart. "Changes in his sex organs are obvious" and his hands perspire. At this point, "some girls experience an all-over relaxation." Duvall explains that stopping is a girl's responsibility because women are less easily excited and more slowly moved to demand sexual contact: "If two lovers are swept off their feet, it is the girl that is blamed. . . . 'She should have known better,' " people will say. However, it is important that a girl know how to make a boy stop without hurting his ego. Several suggestions are incorporated in little anecdotes—for instance, the girl who firmly removes the boy's hand "as she says with mock surprise, 'Why, this isn't Tuesday, is it?' "

How to say no in other difficult situations is the subject of the next chapter—not only how to say no but how to say it with grace and tact so that the smooth surface of social acceptance is not disturbed. Duvall shows how to turn down a drink or a cigarette so that everybody else is still comfortable drinking and smoking, how to refuse to go along with the gang to a questionable night spot without seeming like a prig, how to ask a date to stop drinking so nicely that he will ask for another date, how to handle unwelcome advances or refuse a date without rejecting the person—all useful and appropriate tactics in the context of the times.

"Love under a cloud" explores the pain of loving inappropriately. Crushes on members of one's own sex—which Duvall explains as resulting from delayed emotional development—and on other love objects that parents will not accept (no examples) can be unhappy situations. In a passage remarkable for its rarity in teen sex education, Duvall explores the trauma of falling in love with a married man (the picture shows a babysitter with her employers) or woman. Duvall displays an unusual candor in admitting that this kind of love is quite common, and discusses its understandable appeal and inherent heartache with calm good sense.

Going steady was an inevitable outcome of dating, and one that Duvall and other sex educators looked at askance. Although she acknowledges the benefits of going steady, including the comfort of social security, she is wary about the possibility of the couple becoming "too involved" or the pain of the inevitable breakup. Practical advice for recovering from a broken heart and getting back in circulation is offered to the ex-steady.

Further chapters on the nature of love, getting engaged, and preparing for marriage complete the book. Not until she can set it properly in the context of marriage does Duvall describe the sex act itself, and then only in the most straightforward terms: "Physically it is a relatively simple procedure. After an initial period of sexual excitation, the penis becomes erect and is thrust into the vagina. A series of in and out movements eventuates in the ejaculation of semen from the penis. The woman may or may not have a climax in which her sex tension is released. Following the sexual climax is a period of relaxation and usually sleep."

The first two editions of *Facts of Life and Love* (1950 and 1956) differ in only minor ways. The later edition adds an index, changes the paragraph and chapter headings, and rearranges the material on dating, but the content remains the same. There are a few tiny deletions, such as a reference to "enjoying" a shady reputation and a sentence implying that engagement adjustment predicts marriage adjustment (possibly removed because it might be interpreted as sanctioning sex for engaged couples).

The 1963 edition, however, looks entirely different and has a new title: *Love and the Facts of Life.* The page is larger and the cartoons by Ruth Belew have been replaced with more subtle and dignified drawings. The book opens with a new chapter on feelings and emotional maturity, in which we are told a sad story about a girl who married the first man who came along and found herself a drudge at eighteen. This change of attitude toward early marriage is expanded in the final chapter, where Duvall explains that early marriage (or sex) is unwise and better deferred for ten or twelve years while a young person gets an education: "Too early involvement in irresponsible sexuality stunts growth as a complete human being." A change of attitude is also apparent in the passage on petting. While Duvall still does not approve, she does qualify her disapproval. In answer to "What's the harm?" she allows that it depends on circumstances, such as whether the two people know and love each other or are strangers; whether they are the same age or he grown and she young; and whether "they have high standards of conduct or see themselves as creatures of impulse."

A few minor changes are the inclusion of a caution against carrying "anti-pregnancy pills" for emergencies and the removal of the equivocal passage about the harm of masturbation. Definitions of lesbian, hermaphrodite, and sex change are provided, as are a number of slang terms for prostitute—"easy make," "call girl," "B-girl." The discussion of dating techniques is preserved intact from ten years earlier.

One interesting new feature of the 1963 edition is a chapter called "What do you want to know?" which gives a statistical analysis of the sources of sex information for teens for the years 1938 and 1960. The analysis showed that, in 1938, 30 percent of teenagers got most of their sex information from parents; by 1960 that had risen to 40 percent. Sex education in a religious setting accounted for the knowledge of only 1 percent in 1938 and 3 percent in 1960. The schools were the source for 8 percent in 1938 and (in spite of the furor over sex education classes) exactly the same percentage in 1960. Peers counted for 66 percent of boys' knowledge and 40 percent of girls' in 1938; while the figure for boys declined to 33 percent in 1960, it rose to 50 percent for girls.

The most striking change came in the amount of sex information that was gained from books. In 1938 only 4 percent of young people learned the facts of life from the printed page. By 1960, 33 percent of girls and 25 percent of boys claimed books as their major source of information about sex. Duvall credits this to an increase in the quality and availability of the literature: "A generation and more ago, a young person had a hard time digging out of dictionaries and medical books what he wanted to know about himself and the process of growing up. Now there are a number of books that clearly answer young people's questions about these things in good, wholesome ways." Librarians routinely stock such materials, she explains, for the use of responsible students. Duvall's many titles and editions made up a large section of that stock.

Although the 1963 Love and the Facts of Life was popular, it never attained the classic status of Facts of Life and Love for Teenagers. Librarians in conservative communities still are often faced with requests for that title from teachers who feel that the 1963 changes are just a bit racy for their reading lists.

## A Uniform View

What about the other sex education books of the fifties? Had Duvall swept the field? We have seen that repressive times spur an increase in the production of cautionary advice literature, and this was true of the postwar years. The increased willingness of libraries to purchase sex education books probably also inspired publishers to take advantage of the new market. In any case, there were at least thirty books and countless pamphlets produced between 1948 and 1960.

Although style and format varied, a surprising degree of unanimity prevailed in the content of these works. A brief description of male and female reproductive anatomy was obligatory, as was an explanation of the mechanics of conception, pregnancy, and birth. Most authors expressed at least token approval of natural childbirth. A perfunctory description of sexual intercourse was usual, but only in terms of the male dynamic. Boys were reassured that nocturnal emissions and involuntary erections were normal, and that they should not feel guilty about the sexual imagery in wet dreams. Girls were told that menstruation was not normally painful, but that they should be careful about getting chilled or exercising violently. Sex educators were quick to deny the old tales about masturbation, but just as quick to warn that there is danger in excessive indulgence and in the resulting guilt and shame. They were still horrified at homosexuality, but considered it a sickness curable by psychotherapy. Although there was occasional mention of lesbians, homosexuality was seen as primarily male behavior, and it was usually attributed to fixation at an immature stage of emotional development. Writers continued to warn young boys against the possibility of homosexual seduction and urged them to "report" any older man who approached them.

Dating received warm approval throughout the fifties literature, which described the ritual in varying degrees of detail. Going steady, however, made the sex educators distinctly uneasy, and they pointed out its perils at length. Kissing and necking received reluctant sanction, but petting did not. Petters were warned of the danger of being swept away and the consequences of losing control: pregnancy, venereal disease, abortion, forced marriage. Contraception was mentioned, but only to stress its riskiness, and not until the end of the decade were specific methods described. Girls were invariably reminded of their responsibility for setting limits, not only because they bear the risk of pregnancy but because they were thought to be less easily aroused. In the main, early engagement and marriage were encouraged, although a reaction against this trend began to set in toward the close of the fifties. At that time, too, a few street words—in quotes—began to creep in. There was, of course, almost no acknowledgment of sexual pleasure, although the possibility of orgasm for women was occasionally suggested. However, sex educators remained opposed to premarital intercourse under any circumstances.

# Kinsey's Findings

The overwhelming uniformity of the sex education books of the fifties seems to indicate that they were an accurate reflection of current sexual attitudes. Evidently, this was how middle-class American parents expected their children to behave, and most likely believed they *did* behave. But what was the reality of teenage sexuality? The publication of Alfred Kinsey's monumental *Sexual Behavior in the Human Male* in 1948 and *Sexual Behavior in the Human Female* in 1953 caused a great furor. The disparity between the assumptions of the sex educators and the reality of teen sex behavior as documented by Kinsey was shocking to America's puritanical sensibilities. While teenagers were being told that premarital sex would inevitably lead to terrible consequences, 50 percent of the married women Kinsey interviewed had not been virgins when they married; the figure for married men varied from 60 to 98 percent, depending on educational level. Kinsey reported that one-half to three-quarters of premarital coitus occurred in teenagers' own homes. What is more, 69 percent of the nonvirginal brides had no regrets later, and 13 percent had only minor regrets. Eighty-three percent who became pregnant out of wedlock were not sorry, nor were 16 percent of those who had contracted venereal disease.

Kinsey also found evidence that a significant increase in female sexual activity had taken place during the 1920s; among women born before 1900, 14 percent of those unmarried by age twenty-five had had sexual intercourse; among women born in the next decade, 36 percent of those unmarried by age twenty-five were experienced. Frequency of male intercourse had remained unchanged from Victorian times—the shift took place quite suddenly in women's behavior only. This new trend had not continued to increase but had remained on the same level from 1930 to 1953. Frequency of petting followed a similar pattern, although it was found to be far more common for men among those with higher education. According to Kinsey, masturbation and petting to climax had a clearly beneficial relationship to the degree of satisfaction girls achieved in marital sex: "A major factor in orgasmic marriage for females is premarital orgasmic experience." Among girls who had experienced orgasm before marriage, 45 percent were orgasmic with all marital coitus in the first year of marriage; among the nonexperienced only 25 percent. Most shocking of all, Kinsey found that 37 percent of American males and 28 percent of American females had had or would have at least one homosexual experience between the onset of adolescence and old age. "The facts are complex," he explained carefully, "and can only be understood by focusing on *homosexual behavior* rather than on *homosexual people.*"

America roared with outrage. Energetic attempts were made to discredit Kinsey's methods and motives, and the House Committee on Un-American Activities accused him of espousing the communist doctrine of free love. Like Evelyn Duvall in *Facts of Life and Love*, the sex educators coped in their own way. Many of them reinterpreted Kinsey's findings to their own satisfaction. Regarding homosexuality, for instance, some of them posited a false distinction between normal homosexuality (the kind most people experience) and abnormal homosexuality (the kind that results in perverts). The evidence linking petting to better educated people was taken to mean that college men were too intelligent to risk premarital intercourse. What the sex educators could neither accept nor distort was conveniently ignored and forgotten. Some of Kinsey's data—especially that relating to women's sexual pleasure—has not been fully absorbed into teenage sex instruction to this day.

## Variations on the Fifties Theme

Despite Kinsey, then, the sex education books of the postwar years continued to project a view of normal and acceptable sex behavior that the researcher's finding had largely invalidated. As we have outlined, these books showed a remarkable uniformity of content. A number of titles, however, reflected marginal differences in style and emphasis that throw further light on the attitudes of the times. Let us look at points where some of these books vary, bearing in mind that the similarities far outweigh the differences.

*Teen Days* (1946) by Frances Strain, the author of *Being Born* (1936), is remarkable for its sexism, even in a sexist era. Writing two years after World War II, Strain looks askance at the new independence women had gained by working in defense industries: "As for girls in general they do seem to be edging up on the boys what with their slacks, their flat shoes, their war jobs, the handling of machinery, the driving of trucks, street cars, and other he-man occupations. And how they do love their pay envelopes!" Girls seem to have forgotten, she laments, that there are distinct differences between the sexes: "Many women are not ready to admit these differences. In their desire for equality with men they do not want to recognize them. Again and again a girl will say in speaking of grievances between herself and a sweetheart, 'I wouldn't have done that to him!'

Of course she wouldn't because she is a woman and he is a man." To clarify current thinking about male and female qualities Strain delineates the "Differences between Boy and Girl Nature":

| BOYS | GIRLS |
|---|---|
| Think less of dress | Spend more time and thought on clothes |
| Are less emotional | Are more stormy and tearful |
| Adhere more strictly to principle | "Break over just this once" |
| Keep a secret better | "Don't tell anyone . . ." |
| Have broader interests | Neglect newspapers |
| Are more loyal (even after separation) | Indifferent or resentful after break |
| Are less talkative | Are chatterboxes |
| Are more content in solitude | Can't bear to be alone |
| Have more respect for rights of others | All's fair in love and war |
| Endure pain less well | Seem to have more endurance for pain |
| Are not inclined to nag | Can't stop talking about it |
| Are better spenders | Watch their pennies |
| Are more tolerant | Want to 'make over' a person |
| Are more jealous | Are more possessive |
| Like conservative dress | Like people to notice dress |
| Are more conceited | Watch the looking-glass |
| Are less demonstrative | Are more affectionate |
| Are more direct in approach | Are more tactful |
| Are less orderly around the house | Are more orderly |
| Are more aggressive | Are more yielding |
| Are more forgiving | Hold a grudge longer |
| Are physically more modest | Like to display their charms |
| Love more than one | Love "one and only" |
| Forget about birthdays and anniversaries | Are more sentimental |
| Are more businesslike | Allow personal feelings to enter transactions |
| Stand on their rights | Are more self-sacrificing |
| Make up their minds | Change their minds |

Girls' athletics, Strain feels, should be used to train women in cooperation rather than aggression: "After school, inter-class games take the place of practice for competitive games, the objective being not victory over an adversary but individual development, release from tension, and good-fellowship." Passivity should prevail even in childbirth, the essential female activity: "There are gay little capsules of all colors and kinds which ease the way or put one to sleep. Usually a mother need not concern herself with choices of these medical aids. Her part is to choose a physician whom she can trust . . . and then leave details and methods to him."

Strain is heartily in favor of early dating, feeling that it is good practice for success in marriage. She projects a pyramid of dating progress, "a structure built by American boys and girls themselves in the last few decades," which begins at the base with group dating and proceeds toward the acme of marriage through the stages of double dating, single dating, going steady, courtship, and engagement. Although "there has been too much talk about 'petting' and 'smooching,' " Strain presents a list of "Rules for Conduct" that is more practical than most: do not go drifting off into cosy corners and lover's lanes, avoid blackouts and dimouts, seat the boy in a chair and not on the couch, have interesting things to do, and do not succumb to sighs and tears and ask for comforting.

*Dates and Dating* (1948) by Esther Emerson Sweeney, copyrighted by the National Board of the Young Women's Christian Association, is typical of the pamphlets of courtship etiquette that were produced by many social agencies during this period. Dating is "a testing ground for marriage" and a way to increase one's understanding of people. "Today's dates are tomorrow's brides," but petting and necking are not for the unmarried: "These are actually preparatory love-making steps leading to the complete physical and emotional union of two persons. They are not complete acts in themselves. They can terminate only in tension and frustration."

*The Stork Didn't Bring You!* (1948, 1961) by Lois Pemberton is distinguished by sporadic and awkward attempts at teen slang. Describing the courtship practices of the previous generation, she writes "Saturday night jam sessions were strictly ham from the family's own vocal cords with pop or mom beating a wheezy accompaniment on the old pianola." Following a glossary of scientific sexual terms, she explains that there are other words "no printer prints" and that are not found in any dictionary, so "be good kids then, and stick to the accepted ones, huh?" Pemberton drops the jazzy syntax, however, when she gets down to serious matters—for instance, in defining orgasm: "The climax or ultimate gratification in sexual intercourse. In men, it is the moment of seminal emission. In women, satisfaction is signified by the expansion and contraction of the vaginal walls."

Pemberton is scornful of anyone who does not conform to the approved stereotypes of male and female teenage behavior, characterizing deviants as the overly sex conscious, the wolf, the wallflower, the clinging vine, the gushing goon, the tomboy, the sissy, and "other creeps." She sees such nonconformity as the cause of homosexuality: "Sex and self-consciousness is carried to perverted degrees" by those who are "physically unattractive or have grotesque disabilities. . . . Their twisted minds may lead them into all kinds of unnatural sexual relations with those of their own sex." Nonconformists are also the ones who most often succumb to the temptations of petting: "Over-indulgence in kissing can lead only to the dark corners and the progressive gruesome twosome stages. . . . And it's almost always the unpopular ones who are guilty, and they smooch in defiance at being cast aside socially." As a further deterrent to premarital sex, Pemberton offers this description of abortion: "The curette operation, illegally performed by unethical doctors and untrained midwives at an exorbitant fee . . . consists of opening the cervix and scraping the embryo from the womb. A fearfully painful performance. It'll be done primitively with half-sterilized instruments, in drab surroundings. No anesthesia or kind word accompany it to ease the fears and pain."

Letters to Jane (1948) by Gladys Shultz is a series of missives written by a mother to her daughter at college at the point when "sex rears its ugly head." Jane had been necking with her boyfriend one night when "it turned into something else again. All of a sudden I wasn't myself any more." She tells her mother that although she is still a virgin, she is shocked and surprised at "learning I am not the nice girl I always thought I was." Through the letters Jane's mother sends to her daughter, Shultz works in most of the expected advice on the physical and emotional aspects of sex. Jane shares these letters with the other girls in the dormitory, including one named Shirley, a thin, dark, intense girl with an unhappy face. Shirley advocates free love and a woman's right to have an illegitimate child. Mother, however, sees through this facade and reveals Shirley's underlying insecurity. One kindly letter explains to Shirley and Jane that when a man really loves a woman he wants her for his wife, not as a "make," and that a man wants to feel that he doesn't have to watch his wife all the time. When Jane gets Shirley a date with a friend of her own boyfriend, Shirley's radical opinions melt away. After several more letters, Jane gets engaged, and all ends happily in expectation of a wedding.

*Toward Manhood* (1951) by Herman Bundesen was evidently meant to be a male counterpart of *Letters to Jane*. Although the format differs, both books were published by the same publisher and both use the same drawings of the male and female reproductive systems. Bundesen, who was health commissioner of Chicago, had strong opinions about vice. Sex, he felt, "like hunger, is one of the driving forces of life. It will not be denied. . . .There is no primitive impulse that can work more lasting harm on others, if uncontrolled, than the sex urge." Young people can have a hard time squelching this power: "The boy who wants to be as clean in mind as he is in body may sometimes feel that he is obsessed by lewd devils, which he cannot fight off no matter how hard he tries." Seductive girls— "round-heels" or "teasers"—are "definitely dangerous, however sympathetic one may be because of the origin of their warped and twisted attitudes." Homosexuality is also a menace—"a sign of a sick and twisted personality." Furthermore, "women with a concealed homosexual tendency are incapable of warm, motherly feelings. Their love is selfish."

Like Pemberton, Bundesen emphasizes the dangers of abortion, which, of course, was to remain illegal for another twenty years: "To dislodge a strong, healthy embryo or fetus from the mother's womb is a risky business. Death is very much more likely to result from an operation of this kind than from childbirth." A young woman who has had an abortion may "all the rest of her life blame herself for having done a great wrong, refrain from marriage, and forfeit all chances for a happy family life." There may be suicide attempts, or a "black market" adoption of the baby by an unsuitable couple. A young man is also in for rough going if he "should betray his ideals and has acquired a venereal disease in consequence."

In a first mention of drugs, Bundesen deplores the "unspeakably vicious drug traffic" and the power of those substances to destroy inhibitions. Nor is it much better to frequent "beer joints and bootleg hangouts" (an unlikely event in 1951). Early marriage is a solution to all these problems, even though "in many cases it means that the young wife must drop her college work. The girls don't seem to mind it however. They usually report that they would rather have their baby than a college degree."

A pair of books by Frank Howard Richardson, *For Boys Only* (1952, 1959) and *For Girls Only* (1953, 1960) stand out in their use of particularly affected prose. Each employs the format of a fictional-ized set of chats; the "fellows" are treated to talks at a school chapel by a figure called the Doctor ("We always have a big time at these parties"), and the girls are instructed around the bonfire at summer camp by a misty person called Lady. Lady has little to tell the girls other than the facts of menstruation and how to be clean and charm-ing, and her advice about men is restricted to warnings, as ex-emplified in her story about a "fast" camper who "goes for a ride" with a boy who drives the camp truck. Lady conveys her information about venereal disease in one sentence: "There are certain diseases that are known as the 'social diseases' because they are usually, al-though not always, the direct result of immoral association between men and women." At the end of the book, Lady sits by the dying campfire, well satisfied with her summer's work: "There was a pray-er in her heart that each one would grow into womanhood fully equipped to make the world a better place, and to create a home that America could be proud of."

The Doctor, on the other hand, provides much more anatomical detail for the boys, but in an awkward, conversational fashion. In talking about the sperm's role in conception: "Pretty big jump from a speck so small you can't see it without a microscope, to a big lug like one of you, wasn't it? Now what do you suppose the womb does so that it can take care of such an egg, if it gets fertilized?" In this atmo-sphere of manly camaraderie, the boys get up their courage to ask some questions such as, "I say, doctor, just what is the fun in what the older fellows are always beating their gums about—petting, or necking, or boodling? Is it the same as what the older people used to call spooning?" Another boy asks, "What makes older fellows try to get boys to let them do things to them that they know they ought not to do?" to which the Doctor answers that these people are "mentally 'off' " and should be reported to the authorities. "After all, fellows," the doctor confides as he ends his talk, "there's a lot of satisfaction in being decent, and a good sport, and having the feeling toward girls and women we all know the right sort of boys and men have. We know they're not as strong as we are and so are entitled to our pro-tection: and it just isn't cricket to harm them or make trouble for them. . . . There are lots of ways of having good times with girls. Let's not choose the wrong ones."

*Your Dating Days* (1954) by Paul Landis is an excerpt from a larger work by the same author entitled *Your Marriage and Family Living*. Landis, who was a professor of sociology at the State College of Washington, is primarily interested in discussing preparation for marriage, and his book includes some startling statistics on teen dating from the Purdue Opinion Poll for Young People. Compiled at a time when sex educators were picturing American teenagers as almost unanimously involved in dating and (describing nonpartici-pants as social outcasts), this poll revealed that 48 percent of boys and 39 percent of girls rarely or never went out on dates.

Research findings that indicated frequent premarital intercourse among teenagers were also studiously ignored by many writers. Lester Kirkendall, professor of family life at Oregon State University, researched and wrote a serious adult study on the subject, *Premarital Intercourse and Interpersonal Relationships* (1961). Yet, in his pamphlet for teenagers, *Understanding Sex* (first printed in 1947, revised in 1957, and included in the 1954 and 1966 editions of *How to Be a Successful Teen-ager* by William C. Menninger), he invoked the dangers of pregnancy, venereal disease, and loss of respect as deterrents, and warned young people that "practically all dating relationships in which premarital intercourse occurs fail to continue into engagement and marriage." This warning and advice remained essentially unchanged throughout the successive editions. However, Kirkendall's pamphlet is unique in one way. For the very first time, teenagers are told (after the usual warnings) that it might be all right to be friends with a homosexual: "Many people have homosexual desires, yet know how to control their impulses and never seek to bring others into homosexual practices. Such persons may make as good citizens and as good friends as anyone else."

In 1955, Gladys Shultz, author of *Letters to Jane*, wrote another book, *It's Time You Knew*, addressed to Jane's younger sister. The book has a peculiar glossary, not of scientific terms, but of words and phrases that Shultz thought might be puzzling to young girls, such as *illicit relations* ("less blunt sounding than fornication"), *mistress* ("As you get older, you will realize how very many complications are possible in the relations between the sexes. In this country such arrangements are not condoned or excused"), *promiscuity* ("more is found the lower one goes in the social scale—it is often associated with ignorance"), and *prostitute* ("just about the worst thing a human being can do"). Although Shultz tells Jane's sister that "it is not usual for a girl in the early or middle teens to have very strong sex feelings," this statement is carefully qualified in another chapter: "If a girl at or after puberty is troubled by strong sex drives—an urge to have more than friendly relations with the boys she knows, or to do a good deal of masturbating—then she, too, should seek help.

This is not the usual picture for girls in the early or middle teens, and a sympathetic, up-to-date doctor ought to be consulted. Conceivably, some disturbance of the glands may be responsible, such as overactivity of the pituitary or thyroid."

In 1956, two works that previously had been issued as pamphlets by the American Medical Association and the National Education Association were published in book form—*Learni* about *Love* and *What's Happening to Me?* by Marion Lerrigo and Helen Southard. Although the stated objective of these works was "to support the teen-ager in his intention and desire to live up to ideals of good sex conduct and to avoid actions that may make him feel guilty and unhappy," the books were entirely conventional in content. No one asked why sex was expected to make a teenager feel guilty and unhappy.

Religious sex education books generally followed the thinking of the secular sex educators. Marginal differences in liberality or conservatism reflected the stance of the sponsoring denomination. And, of course, these writers were able to employ the authority of religious dogma and scriptural interpretation to reinforce the fading threats of pregnancy, venereal disease, and social ostracism. *From Teens to Marriage* by Reuben Behlmer was published in 1959 by Concordia (Lutheran) and is fairly typical of midline Protestantism. The first sentence—"You have been wonderfully made by the divine Creator (Psalm 139:14)"—sets the biblical tone. The author extols the virtues of home, family, school, and religion. "The story of life" suffers from a lack of diagrams to clarify the anatomical description (just where *is* the inguinal canal?). After the usual information on birth, menstruation, and masturbation, a detailed guide to dating includes this directive: "If you are one who has never dated, the fault might be yours; if so, correct it." Behlmer interprets the admonition from Exodus 20:14 ("Thou shalt not commit adultery") to forbid both extra- and premarital sex relations, but he reminds transgressors that God forgives all sins (John 8:1–11). A discussion of love, engagement, and marriage cautions against the high divorce risk of marriages between people of unlike faiths, and warns in detail against marrying a Catholic—even giving the full text of the agreement required in such cases.

Some other sex education books with a religious orientation were *Growing Up; A Book for Girls, by a Catholic Woman Doctor* by Mary Kidd (1946), *Life and Love; A Christian View of Sex* by Clyde Marramore (1956), and *God, Sex and Youth* by William Hulme (1959).

## Toward the Sixties

It was not until 1958 that a sex education book was written that began to reflect the sexual revolution that had begun to overtake American society—*Sex and the Adolescent* by Maxine Davis. The author, a magazine writer, was not a member of the sexology establishment, and as such she brought a fresh perspective to the subject. As a journalist, Davis did not attempt to ignore the facts, but there is a certain schizophrenic quality to her work; time and again she verges on new insights, which she then qualifies with older attitudes. Davis puts her subject in historical perspective, as in her discussion of the development of attitudes about masturbation, and her style is warm and anecdotal. In spite of this, the book was never very popular, possibly because of its slight unorthodoxy.

Right at the beginning, Davis breaks with tradition by explaining that although she "employs the vocabulary the doctor uses" for clarity, there are other perfectly good Anglo-Saxon words. Examples are *pee, screw,* and *come.* "For personal use, any term that expresses clearly what one wants to say is a good word." Her description of intercourse, which she explains is "a mere diagram of action," is followed by a passage that gives the first hint of sex as a highly civilized pleasure that increases with skill and care: "Sexual love is a much longer more complicated experience than just the above. It is an art which good men learn later on." The usual advice on masturbation is proffered, with two interesting additions. Davis points out approvingly that a young man may learn to delay his orgasm by masturbating with fantasies. She also raises the problem of religious disapproval—the Roman Catholic Church states specifically that masturbation is "intrinsically evil, being contrary to the Divine and Natural Laws." This can be a problem for the individual who "must reconcile his religious convictions, his sex life, and his whole self." Davis reluctantly acknowledges Kinsey's data on homosexuality— "Today we shudder at new sets of statistics showing how many true homosexuals there are in the country and how many other people have had homosexual experience"—but copes by making the distinction (unfounded in Kinsey's work) between "normal" homosexuality and perversion.

Davis is forthright about women's sexual pleasure. She defines the clitoris as "a small organ designed solely for enjoyment of sexual activity," explaining further that the clitoris "has no other purpose. In times past women either did not know (or else pretended not to know) that it existed." Orgasm, while "not absolutely essential to health or happiness," enables a woman "to share her husband's pleasure." She notes (Kinsey's finding) that although girls are only mildly stimulated from erotica and visual stimuli, some kinds of "personal contact will arouse a surge of desire so intense that it requires expression and release." She describes techniques of female masturbation, such as finger and thigh pressure, and warns that girls who masturbate without climax may form the habit of self-suppression and be unable to find satisfaction in married sex. About petting she is generally disapproving but admits that it is something that "everybody does"—"an almost universal practice" that "helps a young person learn about his own desires and those of the opposite sex," adding that this is "especially important for girls."

Unlike earlier sex educators, Davis discusses (albeit negatively) the possibility of petting to orgasm: "Steadies who pet may develop techniques for finding gratification and reaching orgasm without intercourse and thereby establish a sexual pattern that may interfere later with the far deeper satisfaction of complete union in marriage." She owns up to the findings of "responsible studies" that many women have sex before marriage, and allows that "girls who do" are no longer outcasts. Because in illicit sex boys are liable to be hasty and inconsiderate, however, "for a girl it is not likely to be genuinely pleasurable."

Although Davis warns that contraceptives give "a sense of security for which there is very little foundation," she does describe the condom, the diaphragm, the rhythm method, and withdrawal in some detail. She credits Kinsey for some statistics indicating that the consequences of abortion "may not be so dire as supposed" and states that, although these operations are illegal, some abortionists may be competent and responsible. Still, at this point, she cannot resist including a vivid horror story about a visit to an abortionist. However clearly such passages locate *Sex and the Adolescent* within the literature of its decade, Davis's book unmistakably points toward the relaxation of attitudes that would become increasingly evident in the sex education books of the sixties.

## BIBLIOGRAPHY

Behlmer, Reuben D. *From Teens to Marriage*. St. Louis, MO: Concordia Publishing House, 1959.
Brecher, Edward M. *The Sex Researchers*. Boston: Little, Brown, 1969.
Bundesen, Herman N. *Toward Manhood*. Philadelphia: Lippincott, 1951.
Davis, Maxine. *Sex and the Adolescent*. New York: Dial, 1958.

Duvall, Evelyn Ruth Millis. *About Sex and Growing Up.* New York: Association Press, 1968.

———. *The Art of Dating.* New York: Association Press, 1958, rev. ed., 1967.

———. *Facts of Life and Love for Teenagers.* New York: Association Press, 1950, rev. ed., 1956.

———. *Love and the Facts of Life.* New York: Association Press, 1963.

———. *Today's Teen-agers.* New York: Association Press, 1966.

———. *Why Wait Till Marriage?* New York: Association Press, 1965.

———. and Duvall, Sylvanus Milne. *Sense and Nonsense about Sex.* New York: Association Press, 1962.

———, eds. *Sex Ways—In Fact and Faith.* New York: Association Press, 1961.

Duvall, Evelyn Ruth Millis, and Hill, Reuben. *When You Marry.* New York: Association Press, 1945; Lexington, MA: Heath, rev. ed., 1953, high school eds., 1962, 1967.

Duvall, Sylvanus Milne. *Before You Marry; 101 Questions to Ask Yourself.* New York: Association Press, 1959.

———. *101 Questions to Ask Yourself before You Marry.* New York: Association Press, 1950.

Hulme, William Edward. *God, Sex and Youth.* Englewood Cliffs, NJ: Prentice-Hall, 1959.

Kidd, Mary. *Growing Up; A Book for Girls, by a Catholic Woman Doctor.* New York: Benziger Bros., 1946.

Kinsey, Alfred C. et al. *Sexual Behavior in the Human Female.* Philadelphia: Saunders, 1953.

Kinsey, Alfred C., Pomeroy, Wardell B., and Martin, Clyde E. *Sexual Behavior in the Human Male.* Philadelphia: Saunders, 1948.

Kirkendall, Lester Allen. *Premarital Intercourse and Interpersonal Relationships.* New York: Julian Press, 1961.

———. *Understanding Sex.* Chicago: Science Research Associates, 1947, rev. ed., 1957.

Landis, Paul H. *Your Dating Days; Looking Forward to Happy Marriage.* New York: McGraw-Hill (Whittlesey House), 1954.

Lerrigo, Marion Olive, and Southard, Helen. *Learning about Love; Sound Facts and Healthy Attitudes toward Sex and Marriage.* New York: Dutton, 1956.

———. *What's Happening to Me?* New York: Dutton, 1956.

Marramore, Clyde M. *Life and Love; A Christian View of Sex.* Grand Rapids, MI: Zondervan, 1956.

Menninger, William C. et al. *How to Be a Successful Teen-ager.* New York: Sterling, 1954, 1966.

Pemberton, Lois Loyd. *The Stork Didn't Bring You!* New York: Hermitage Press, 1948, New York: Nelson, rev. ed., 1961.

Richardson, Frank Howard. *For Boys Only; The Doctor Discusses the Mysteries of Manhood.* Atlanta: Tupper & Love, 1952, 1959.

————. *For Girls Only; The Doctor Discusses the Mysteries of Womanhood.* Atlanta; Tupper & Love, 1953, 1960.

Shultz, Gladys Denny. *It's Time You Knew.* Philadelphia: Lippincott, 1955.

————. *Letters to Jane.* Philadelphia: Lippincott, 1948.

Strain, Frances Bruce. *Teen Days.* New York: Appleton-Century-Crofts, 1946.

Sweeney, Esther Emerson. *Dates and Dating.* Whiteside, NY: Woman's Press, 1948.

# 7

# *The Sexual Revolution*

While the youth of the sixties were exploring the outer limits of reality with LSD, protesting the Vietnam War, marching in civil rights demonstrations, and making love not war, the sex educators of that decade wrote dozens of books that attempted to keep the lid on a sexual revolution that already was well underway. The one significant difference between the books of the sixties and those of the fifties was a growing but reluctant recognition of women's sexuality, as cautious references to the clitoris as the source of sexual pleasure for women became more frequent. However, there were still a few last gasps from the proponents of the repressive attitudes toward women so characteristic of the postwar years.

One such writer was Dr. Bernhardt Gottlieb. Although his 1960 book for young men, *What a Boy Should Know about Sex*, is unremarkable except for the unconscious echo of Sylvanus Stall in the title, Gottlieb's book for young women, *What a Girl Should Know about Sex* (1961), is exceptional in its emphasis on "a feminine characteristic called passivity." With warm approval Gottlieb describes the deliberate muffling of a young girl's humanity: "The first impulse of the young adolescent girl is opposition to everything and everybody, . . . a display of aggression, a protest against discipline and control. But then something happens. The girl quietly changes and somehow loses her battling attitude. Gradually she becomes sweet, docile, and agreeable. From the active, assertive adolescent she gradually changes into a passive young woman." Furthermore, "her feminine trait of self-effacement is ever present. It gives her satisfaction." This becomes important later in meeting the demands of a husband: "His mother attended to the household chores and to his personal needs. Now that he has a home of his own, he expects his wife to take on many of the tasks that his mother performed."

In fact, as Gottlieb sees it, women's maternal functions dominate not only their relationships with their husbands but everything they do in life: "Their first interest is to become a mother. Every other interest in life becomes less important. A woman's motherliness is ever present even in her interests of college, job, or professional career. Her place of employment becomes a second home to her. She thinks how nice it would be to have flowers on the desk and appropriate pictures on the walls, so that others who come to her little nook will feel her warmth." On the subject of childbirth, he declares, "It is as though woman instead of man was made to suffer in order to obtain certain satisfactions and pleasures." And, in closing, "Maternal love demands nothing, sets no limits, makes no reservations."

In contrast, *What Teenagers Want to Know* (1962) by Florence Levinsohn is forthright about discussing the confusion women face in making new role choices and meeting society's traditional expectations for them. Like other sex educators of the time, she deplores the new climate of sexual indulgence: "Advertising, television, movies, and novels often lead an adolescent to think that sexual experience must be the key to glamour and romance, the road to a new world of importance and strength." But the rules say wait, she reminds teenagers. Peer group pressure is a strong influence on sexual attitudes, but parents want their sons and daughters to remain virgins until married. Levinsohn acknowledges the strain created by these conflicting pressures and notes that they may produce extreme attitudes on either end of the scale: "All the circumstances may combine to create strong inhibitions, to prevent [a young man or woman] from any sexual experimentation at all. At the other extreme, the circumstances may combine to lead to a great deal of sexual experience, to promiscuity, often in the form of conquests." Both attitudes call for professional help, she says.

## Sex Prevention in the Sixties

In 1963, the same year that the third edition of Evelyn Duvall's *Love and the Facts of Life* was published, Ann Landers organized her opinions on the subject in a book that was based on her syndicated newspaper column. *Ann Landers Talks to Teen-agers about Sex* is studded with anecdotes, examples, and object lessons from her mailbag. From the statistical sampling that her correspondents provided, Landers must have been well aware that many teenagers were no longer automatically following the behavioral codes they had inherited. The introduction addressed to parents speaks of teenagers "pulled and hauled by biological urges on the one hand and fear of the consequences on the other." Yet, in the body of the book, she offers teenagers no help with the conflict. Sex outside of marriage is "unacceptable in our society" and "it isn't worth the risks." Sex on the sly makes a girl feel "cheap, dirty and disgusted with the boy," and teenage boys are "undisciplined and awkward" lovers.

　She has sharp words for those who feel that some practical advice might be in order: "Every now and then I get a letter from some knuckle-head who tells me if I really want to befriend teen-agers, I should give them some helpful hints on how to avoid pregnancy instead of being so doggone puritanical and unrealistic." There is no foolproof method of birth control anyway, Landers retorts. By way of a "helpful hint," she suggests sublimation—athletics for boys and housework for girls. An abstainer from alcohol herself, Landers emphasizes the evils of drink, but she is humane and wise in discussing kind ways to break up with a steady without causing too much pain. Her advice on venereal disease is also practical and sympathetic for 1963; she advises teenagers to go to a family doctor or city or county health department for treatment and ask them not to contact their parents; they may not, although there is no guarantee, because some states require that parents be notified.

The many desperate letters Landers had received from boys who suspected they were homosexual had made her aware of the emotion surrounding that subject. In her book she explains that nobody understands the cause of homosexuality, but details several lurid case histories illustrating popular theories about it. She admits that transvestites and child molesters are not homosexual and adds that "many homosexuals are content as they are and have no wish to change. They are not a problem to society or to themselves." However, Landers concludes that "most homosexuals yearn to be normal" because they are "twisted and sick"; unfortunately, only about 4 out of 100 can be made heterosexual. "God meant sex to be pleasurable, beautiful, filled with wonder and rich in reward" she rhapsodizes, "but—only if it is used properly." To the girl who wrote that her amorous boyfriend was "fed up with the broken record" of her resistance, Landers replies "That broken record produces darned fine music. Just keep telling him to behave himself . . . behave himself . . . behave himself. . . ."

Two books that were also far behind the times were *Moving into Manhood* (1963) and *The Way to Womanhood* (1965) by William Bauer, who was then the director of health education for the American Medical Association. Bauer begins his advice to young men by expounding the Victorian doctrine of seminal conservation: "Your sex is what makes you a man. Its influence upon you is not only physical, but spiritual and emotional. Physically, your sex makes you strong and ambitious. Your sex also makes you a leader because it gives you the impulses and the qualities which make for leadership." Masturbation, he states, is "almost always accompanied by an instinctive sense of guilt or at least of shame." Regarding drugs, Bauer warns: "The smoking of so-called 'reefers' is practiced in certain areas by some young people and is admittedly a serious evil. Marijuana users become irresponsible and get themselves into trouble by doing things which they would never have dreamed of doing in their right senses. This includes sexual misconduct. Often the body's demand for drugs leads to robbery, blackmail, or even murder."

In *The Way to Womanhood* Bauer is joined by his wife, Florence, as coauthor ("Just call us Polly and Bill"). Together they agree that "marriage and motherhood is woman's most important role in life. A career should be secondary." To that end, the way to attract boys is to be nonchalant and save physical expression of affection for special moments, as "when he really does delight you." At these times a girl should show her feelings "in unexpected ways, such as grabbing both his hands and whirling around with him, or giving him a quick hug and dancing away." This exercise of restraint should not be too hard because "sexual desire in a girl may not come until after her marriage. In some women it never comes. Such a lack is rarely known to a boy or man."

According to the Bauers, painful menstruation may be caused by "a girl's unconscious rebellion against being a girl." They are stern about abortion—it is "cold, calculated murder of the child and often endangers or takes the life of the mother"—and they take a firm stand against premarital sex and any other violation of traditional sexual mores: "The real reason that any irregular sexual life should be avoided is that it is wrong. It is wrong morally, religiously, socially, medically, and biologically; in every one of these fields it violates the fundamental experience of the race through many centuries."

Similarly, Bertrand Glassberg writes in *Barron's Teen-age Sex Counselor* (1965) that "Even the Godless Communists are becoming doubtful of the wisdom of permitting free sexual relationships." In answer to the question "Is the hymen ever broken without intercourse having taken place?" Glassberg is not reassuring ("very rarely" he says), and when asked "Why can't teenagers use contraceptives?" he declares that "Contraceptives are intended for the use of husbands and wives." Other books of the same year and type were *Youth Considers Sex* by William Edward Hulme, *Love, Sex, and the Teenager* by Rhoda Lorand, *Not While You're a Freshman* by Helen Walker Puner, *Adolescent Freedom and Responsibility* by Gerald J. Taylor, and the third edition of *The Stork Didn't Bring You!* by Lois Pemberton. In addition, two religious sex education books were published in 1965—*Learning to Love* by Marc Oraison and the revised edition of *Sex and the Whole Person* by Frank Wier.

However, another sex education book published in 1965 was a different matter. This was *Love and Sex in Plain Language* by Eric W. Johnson. With its spare and simple style and emphasis on human communication, it can be seen as the first of the modern sex education books. Frequent later editions (1967, 1973, 1977) kept abreast of rapid changes in attitudes and scientific knowledge, and the last edition (to be examined in detail in Chapter 8) is still in use. In 1965 Johnson was headmaster of the Friends' Central School in Philadelphia. Although *Love and Sex in Plain Language* is not radically different in content from most books that preceded it, Johnson's clear writing, his empathy for teenagers' feelings, and his sense of organization make it outstanding.

The book is addressed to junior high teenagers, but, as Johnson points out, it could be used by bright ten-year-olds as well as college age youth. The chapters proceed logically from "The man's part in love and sex" and "The woman's part in love and sex" to "Sexual intercourse," "The baby from fertilization to birth," "How a baby is born and what a newborn is like," through chapters on the differences between human sex and animal sex, birth control, and love. In 68 pages, Johnson conveys more information than other books three times its size. The sepia ink drawings by Edward C. Smith are informative and often very beautiful: one illustration depicting three nude boys of vastly different stages of sexual development demonstrates "normal teen-age boys of the same age"; another pair of drawings shows the moment of the fertilization and the path of the egg to the uterus.

Like his contemporaries, Johnson calls homosexuality a sickness (although he does not associate it with child molesting) and is sure that the frequent masturbator will be prey to guilt, shame, and social isolation. Although he does dwell on the unfortunate circumstances of illegitimate pregnancy and venereal disease, his primary reason for urging teenagers not to undertake sexual intercourse too lightly is a respect for people, who, he emphasizes, "are not made to be used."

Sex without deep caring can also cause guilt and shame, which may spoil later experiences.

Johnson lays out rigid role expectations for the sexes: "A typical boy is vigorous and aggressive; a typical girl is sweeter and gentler than he and has a greater desire to please others. A father is expected to earn a living for his family and to provide manly companionship for his wife and children. On the other hand, a mother, even if she helps to earn a living for the family, provides loving care for her children, manages the household and is a source of tenderness and womanly love."

The greatest fault of *Love and Sex in Plain Language*, but one that was remedied in later editions, is the inadequate description of female sexuality. There is no drawing of female external genitalia, and no explanation of the function of the clitoris. Although Johnson does say that intercourse is "one of the greatest pleasures mankind enjoys," he offers a description that, while admirable in other ways, is entirely from the male point of view:

> Some couples may have sexual intercourse several times a week, others perhaps only once or twice a month. Intercourse may take anywhere from a few minutes to half an hour or more. The couple come together and usually kiss, embrace and caress each other. Often they tell their love for each other. After a time, the woman's mind and body become prepared for the act of coitus; her vagina becomes moist and soft. Meanwhile, and much more quickly, the man's penis has become erect so that it enters the vagina easily. After a time of moving back and forth, the husband and wife reach the climax of sexual pleasure, called an orgasm. For the husband, this is the moment when the semen is ejaculated inside the vagina in a series of quick spurts toward the neck of the uterus. For the woman, the orgasm is a series of muscular contractions of the walls of the vagina. There is no secretion of fluid like that of the ejaculation of semen in a man. Husband and wife rather seldom experience orgasm at the same moment during intercourse. Indeed, some women rarely or never experience orgasm but still enjoy intercourse. After the climax of intercourse, the couple feel close, loving and relaxed.

Johnson devotes a whole chapter to birth control. Voicing a concern for world overpopulation, he says, "In recent years, almost all thoughtful people in this country have come to agree that family planning is a necessity." The main discussion now is about which method to use. He notes that even Catholics accept the need for birth limitation and permit it if the means used are natural. In the framework of marriage he discusses abstinence, the diaphragm, the condom, chemicals, the pill, the coil, rhythm, and sterilization, and notes that it is important to follow a doctor's advice to ensure the effectiveness of most birth control methods. In a final chapter on love, Johnson reiterates his theme: "Never forget that human beings are not made to be used, but rather to be understood, appreciated, loved and deeply respected. Physical love is a part—but only a part—of such understanding and respect."

Taking advantage of the booming sex education market, in 1966 the Public Affairs Committee, an independent research organization, brought together seven of its previously published pamphlets in a book titled *Teen Love, Teen Marriage*. Some of the material included dated back as far as 1950, and bore the marks of an earlier era—pamphlets on dating by Paul Landis and Ralph Eckert, for instance. However, the last item, "Let's Talk Sense about Sex!" by Lester Kirkendall with Elizabeth Ogg, is an unusual piece that was originally written for adults but is included in the book as if for teens. The authors discuss changing and multiple cultural patterns that make "none of us . . . sure that our traditional sex code is 'right.' " The central moral issue, they tell grown-ups, is the quality of the relationship, not the degree of genital activity.

Also in 1966, a book appeared that challenged many long-held beliefs and assumptions about human sexuality. *Human Sexual Response* by William Masters and Virginia Johnson was a monumental collection of observed data on the sex act. Among other things, Masters and Johnson's research indicated that women's capacity for sexual enjoyment was much greater than earlier studies had found; the book fundamentally changed the way women regarded their bodies and their sex lives. The following year, when researchers at the Institute for Sex Research at Indiana University were employed by the Chicago-based National Opinion Research Center to survey the sexual behavior patterns of a random sample of college students, they found that the patterns of the forties and fifties had remained almost unchanged, with one significant difference: in the sixties a much larger proportion of girls were enjoying their first experience with coitus.

Nevertheless, warners and doomsayers continued to be heard. A rambling and uninformed book by Wade V. Lewis, *Sex: in Defense of Teen-agers* (1967), blames the drug scene for the breakdown of moral standards: "*U.S. News and World Report* describes a recent drug craze and its dangers. It is not confined to 'beatniks' but is permeating the colleges, even the high schools." Lewis implies that even a girl who drinks soda is not safe—her date may sneak knock-out drops into her drink for nefarious sexual reasons.

Even more peculiar is *Young People and Sex* (1967) by Arthur H. Cain. The book was one of a series of titles by Cain covering "young people and . . ."—just about every topic, from smoking to jobs. In *Young People and Sex*, Cain offers his eccentric opinions on some of the most complicated and controversial aspects of sexuality. Sexual customs and attitudes have been changing at an unprecedented speed, he states. The resulting confusion has been "expressed in a tendency to close the gap between the sexes." It is becoming hard to tell the boys from the girls—especially since the latter are turning into "intellectual eunuchs." Petting, he claims, can cause infection in the girl and strain the sexual organs of the boy. Postponement of sex is "infinitely preferable."

A chapter on "Sexual customs and attitudes in other countries" soon deteriorates into a superficial look at the status of prostitution in the world's major cities. Cain declares that the most moral states are those where prostitution is legal; in areas where women have been instrumental in getting the practice outlawed, sexual chaos reigns. He holds up Switzerland as an example of a country where there is good sexual order, because the women are beautiful and don't vote. He defines normal sexual behavior as mutual orgasm in the act of intercourse, and then launches into an unconsciously lascivious examination of "abnormal" behaviors and conditions: vaginismus (painful contractions of the vagina), impotency, oral-genital sex, sodomy, coprolalia (involuntary use of obscene language for sexual gratification), and group sex. His fiercest scorn is reserved for homosexuals. "No homosexual behavior can under any circumstances or from any point of view be regarded as normal," and he dismisses the "alleged sex education" that condones homosexuality. Cain describes the "sissified 'pansy' or 'swish' " and points out indignantly: "To most normal men the objectionable thing about these unfortunate people is that they almost always insist perversely on flagrantly intruding their incongruous behavior into societies that regard it as fundamentally insulting." For the problem of pornography he offers a novel solution—high school seniors should take a course in the subject so that they become thoroughly weary of it and it ceases to be forbidden fruit.

More traditional in its approach to sex prevention was *Sex before Twenty: New Answers for Youth* (1967, 1971) by Helen Elizabeth Southard. The author had written a number of sex education pamphlets for the American Medical Association with coauthor Marion Lerrigo and was a psychologist and family life specialist for the Young Women's Christian Association. Southard admits that "a woman can have a climax also, although she does not always experience it because her sexual responses are different from those of men." She finds masturbation infantile, and homosexuality a normal developmental stage that confirmed homosexuals "might grow out of if they didn't feel that they were born that way." But Southard gives her greatest attention to the perils of premarital sex, which she relates to almost every subject she takes up.

Published in 1967, the misnamed *Every Girl's Book of Sex* by Arlette Fribourg was actually a stilted gynecology primer for women of all ages. Its vocabulary ("brassière," "toilette," "swim in the sea") suggested that the author may have been European. Just as odd, but in a refreshing way, was *Dear Doctor Hip Pocrates; Advice Your Family Doctor Never Gave You* (1968). The author, Eugene Schoenfeld, had written a column of medical advice for the underground newspaper, the *Berkeley Barb*, during the height of the sexual and political turmoil in that college community. The book is a collection of letters to that column, many of them poignant, funny, startling, or simply weird. Mixed in with queries about the hallucinogenic properties of various substances, descriptions of bizarre sexual problems, and treatments of mace poisoning is some sound sexual advice. Whether discussing the legal status of abortion, the effectiveness of various contraceptive methods, the long-term results of going braless, or the use of masturbation as a remedy for menstrual cramps, Dr. Hip provides bits of information unavailable in other sex education books for teenagers. In an uncharacteristically serious moment, he sums up the sexual situation of the late sixties: "Two views prevail today. One is to concentrate on loving the person. The other holds that the act itself should be paramount. The most fulfilling and difficult way is to do both."

As the decade drew to a close, most sex educators held to their established themes or opinions, or changed them only slightly. The jazzy pink cover of *A Girl's Guide to Dating and Going Steady* by Tom McGinnis (1968) belied the book's contents—a diatribe against sexual expression outside marriage, with no physiology at all and very little other information that didn't focus on the moral. The author of *The Stork Is Dead* (1968), Charlie Shedd, was an elderly minister of a large church in Texas, who for several years had written a column on sex and love for *Teen* magazine. In his book, he stresses the differences between the ever-ready male and the emotionally needy female, and gives examples of "lines guys use to get a young

thing to go further." Shedd lists reasons (none he considers justifiable) that girls give in, and draws a sorry picture of what it is like to
be married at seventeen. In a chapter titled "Strange things that
might happen," he talks of petting to orgasm as "almost too weird to
describe" and warns that participants might get "fixated" and never
be able to enjoy intercourse. Oral sex is all right in marriage, but
"does more harm than good in pre-marital relationships," and anal
sex is neurotic. As for homosexuals, "turn them over to God" and
walk away. Masturbation can be very bad when it is compulsive, but
"teenage masturbation is preferable to teenage intercourse," and
seen in that light it can be regarded as a gift of God. If you must have
sex, he says—bowing to the inevitable—use birth control. He recommends foam and a condom. But if a relationship has reached that
point, it would be far better for the couple to stop seeing each other
entirely.

Helen Jean Burn, head writer for the Maryland Educational Cultural Broadcasting Commission, revived the question-and-answer
format in her 1969 title, *Better than the Birds, Smarter than the Bees;
No-nonsense Answers to Honest Questions about Sex and Growing
Up.* Some of Burn's supposedly no-nonsense answers would not
have been out of place in the books from the turn of the century.
When asked the best method of birth control, she replies "Don't have
sexual intercourse." Girls are told that an "illegal abortionist may
use a rusty coat hanger or a knitting needle or anything else he has
handy." Regarding the temptation to masturbate, Burns advises teenagers to use that "push" to excel in other things; spending time alone
in one's room is a waste, anyway—better to have a hobby.

An unusual but chilling and Machiavellian book was 'Ellen
Peck's *How to Get a Teen-age Boy and What to Do with Him when
You Get Him* (1969). This had little to say about physical sex, but a
great deal to say about the relations between the sexes. Peck provides
girls with a detailed guide to the techniques of manipulating conversation and using psychology in order to "get" boys. Girls are taught
to lie, dissemble, double deal, and betray their friends in order to get
next to an interesting male. Peck's position on petting is thoroughly
expedient—go slow on "making out," she advises, because that will
keep a boy interested longer.

## Religious Texts

Throughout the decade, as secular authorities became more accepting of masturbation and birth control, Catholic educators react-
ed by issuing a number of books that stressed the sinfulness of these

activities. *The Catholic Youth's Guide to Life and Love* (1960) by the Very Reverend Monsignor George Kelly is fairly typical. The book carries the nihil obstat and the imprimatur of the church, certifying it "free of doctrinal or moral error." "By following the teachings of the Church, you can always know that you're on the right path," says Monsignor Kelly. A chapter on physical sex by James T. Geddis, M.D., explains "It's a fact that acts of self-love cause great spiritual and emotional harm in addition to being sins against the Sixth Commandment." Remedy for this temptation can be sought by "receiving the sacraments daily and saying your daily prayers." A description of the transmission of venereal disease blames not only intercourse but towels and glasses or cups in a public place (although the shared communion vessel is not mentioned).

Kelly stresses the importance of chastity to the family and home. He discourages early dating and especially kissing, because there is "a real danger that the friendship you feel will burst out and overwhelm you, leaving your defenses open to sin." Other chapters examine "Why artificial birth control is wrong" (he quotes Pope Pius XI, who called it "shameful and intrinsically vicious"), "Do you have a religious vocation?," "The spiritual and emotional dangers of marrying a non-Catholic," "Marriage for life," and "The single vocation."

A second book by George Kelly, *Dating for Young Catholics* (1963), was extracted from a series of articles written in 1961 for *Hi-Time*, a religious magazine. Here he exhorts young people to date only Catholics and to struggle with the temptation to commit sins of impurity. He considers the use of birth control to be selfishly motivated, although he allows that the rhythm method is acceptable for very pressing reasons such as health. Other Catholic sex education books included a translation of Marc Oraison's *Learning to Love* (1965), which contained a thoughtful attempt to put the dogma on birth control into perspective, and *A Boy's Sex Life; A Handbook of Basic Information and Moral Guidance* (1969) by William J. Bausch.

Protestant groups also were producing their own sex education texts during the sixties. The Methodist point of view, for instance, was presented in *Sex and the Whole Person: A Christian View* (1962, 1965) by Frank E. Wier, and *Love, Sex, and Life* (1964, 1966) by Marjory Bracher discussed the Lutheran position. The Concordia Sex Education series, also Lutheran, included *Take the High Road* by A. J. Bueltmann (1967) and *Life Can Be Sexual* by Elmer N. Witt (1967). Richard Hettlinger spoke from the liberal Episcopal perspective in *Living with Sex: The Student's Dilemma* (1966), a book for older teenagers and college students; and the Unitarian Church was represented in *Commonsense Sex: A Basis for Discussion and Reappraisal* by Ronald Mazur (1968).

# A New Approach: Positive, Nonjudgmental

The more modern and less didactic sex education books of the seventies were anticipated in 1969 by Paul Bohannan's *Love, Sex, and Being Human*. An anthropologist, Bohannan made an attempt to show teenagers how to "devise their own moralities." "I am not advocating any specific moral behavior," he says, but "I have some values of my own that sometimes show." Using examples from other societies and frequent quotes from Masters and Johnson, he explains that the association between sex and love is not natural and "normal," but a learned cultural value. Furthermore, he points out that "masturbation is a source of consolation, pleasure, and relief of tension before it is possible to link one's sexuality with love and with a loved person." He has an unusual theory about the origin of homosexual patterns: "Confirmed, constant, and habitual homosexuality . . . always arises from some difficulty in the formation of the learned capacity to love, or from inability to esteem one's self highly enough to think one is lovable." The book never gained wide readership, perhaps because of Bohannan's formidable style.

A truly radical work from the same year, and the first book that really approached sex for teenagers in a positive way, was Dr. Eleanor Hamilton's *Sex before Marriage: Guidance for Young Adults, Ages 16–20*. In spite of its ground-breaking nature, the book failed to create a furor because teachers and librarians chose to dismiss it as being meant for the college student, ignoring the clear indication in the title that it was also addressed to younger people.

Hamilton's perspective in *Sex before Marriage* is to consider sex as an integral part of the whole spectrum of bodily pleasures. Masturbation, she writes, has an important function in the ongoing process of developing sexual awareness and responses while growing up. It is "nature's way of preparing you for the later enjoyment of sexuality with a partner" and is a useful release from tension. Furthermore, it is not really possible to masturbate "too much," because the body sets its own limits: "A person who has learned how to come to orgasm through masturbation is much more likely to be a good sex partner in marriage than one who has not." Her objection to petting is not that it is done, but that it is not done well: "If two teenagers do decide to pet, they would be wise to see to it that each comes to orgasm." A pattern of arousal without satisfaction can set bad precedents; girls, for example, can be adversely affected by always having to switch on the red light. However, many women, she reveals, find manual orgasms more satisfying than intercourse, and there is nothing wrong with this: "The word clitoris comes from the Greek word for key, and the clitoris is, indeed, like a magic key to sexual satisfaction for the female."

Hamilton is forthright in explaining that adults have deliberately instilled a fear of sex in young people: "It helps in dissipating guilt if you realize that many of the religious precepts denying sex pleasure to the unmarried are based on conditions which existed at a time long in the past. Their continuance into the present is superstition and reflects not only ignorance of scientific technology but faulty knowledge of the social psychology of today." She tells teenagers quite bluntly that "virginity is about as useful in a prospective wife as an appendix," and adds that "ninety five percent of the dangers of premarital sex could be eliminated if parents would make their homes and their own knowledge available to their children as they would in all other areas of life."

In addition to giving the facts about methods of birth control, Hamilton explores what was then known about the complex psychological factors involved in its use. She is adamant about the need to change abortion laws, and feels that it is preferable to spend money on a trip to Japan or England for a legal operation rather than chance an encounter with an illegal abortionist in the United States. She provides a sympathetic chapter of helpful advice for the unmarried girl who decides to go through with her pregnancy. In a discussion of drugs (an inexplicably rare topic in most other sex education books in that decade of chemical experimentation), she frowns on LSD for good reason, but, in referring to the most common drug, says, "If marijuana is legitimized (as many people believe it will be), it may be added to the list of mild pleasures enjoyed by man—sensual, though not necessarily sexual." She minimizes the risk of venereal disease—there is very little chance of contracting it, she says, if partners are selective—but is more concerned about the very common and seldom discussed female genital infections of monilia and trichomoniasis. Hamilton's comforting words were spread further, when *Sex before Marriage* appeared in paperback in 1973, followed by another book for younger teenagers *Sex, with Love* (which is described in Chapter 9).

A third landmark book after Stall's *What a Young Boy Ought to Know* (1897) and Duvall's *Facts of Life and Love for Teenagers* (1950) was *Boys and Sex* (1968), written by Wardell Pomeroy with collaborator John Tebbel. Pomeroy was uniquely qualified to speak to teenagers about sex. As Alfred Kinsey's associate, and later as director of the Institute for Sex Research, he had conducted thousands of interviews on the subject with young people. His research had made him aware of the hiatus between accepted sexual attitudes and actual sexual behavior in our society. Consequently his approach in *Boys and Sex*, and its companion volume *Girls and Sex* (1969), was to talk to teenagers in a helpful way about the behavior he knew perfectly well was going on, but to remind them that, while they were entitled to their own choices and their own privacy, they would have to deal with the disapproval of adults unless they were discreet.

In the introduction to *Boys and Sex*, intended to reassure parents, Pomeroy states his purpose. Other books for teenagers on sex, he explains, have been "too moralistic, too judgmental, or lacking in forthrightness." Proposing to remedy that lack, he says soothingly, "I am not suggesting in these pages that your sons engage in sexual behavior of any kind. The reality, of course, is that the vast majority of them have already engaged in sex behavior of one kind or another. Once this reality is acknowledged and faced, the next question is, What's going to be done about it!" He encourages parents to talk to their children about sex casually and often, and lists the range of possible attitudes toward sexuality. Fitting himself into that scale, he lays out his own credo: "Sex is pleasurable, and . . . it cannot be denied until we are in our twenties or later. One must show a concern for the other person who may be involved in an act and, moreover, one must learn to live in our society, which is basically antisexual." He declares his own belief in marriage and his advocacy of sexual attitudes and behavior that "help us to make the best possible sexual adjustment in marriage." Helping teenagers to develop healthy attitudes, he feels, is more important than providing them with detailed biological information, and this is what he plans to concentrate on in *Boys and Sex*.

Pomeroy disavows himself as an authority and gives the young readers permission to think for themselves in the very first pages. People disagree about sex, he says, and that's all right. It's even all right to disagree with him—this is not a book of advice. The most important thing to get clear right at the start is a "a fundamental fact

which often seems to be overlooked by those who talk about sex—
that sex is one of the most pleasurable activities available to human
beings." In the obligatory chapter on anatomy and physiology that
follows, he is "deliberately sketchy" (he uses scientific terms here
but defines the street words in a later section). Pomeroy is more interested in behavior, and soon gets down to discussing the kinds of
sexual activity with which most boys are already familiar from experience. People are born sexual beings, he explains, and even babies
have sexual feelings. Almost everybody has been involved in epi-
sodes of sex play before adolescence (he gives statistics) and it is
nothing to be ashamed of, even though parents usually disapprove
strongly.

Pomeroy attempts an objective approach to masturbation, giving
a list of pros and cons, but it is immediately apparent where his
sympathies lie, and he soon gives up the pose and admits that it is
"not only harmless, but is positively good and healthy, and should
be encouraged because it helps young people to grow up sexually in
a natural way." He explains the variations in technique, for both
boys and girls, and praises it as a way for a boy to learn to delay his
orgasm—a skill that is useful later in intercourse.

Homosexuality also is given thoughtful and informed consideration. He traces the historical origins of Judeo-Christian attitudes
toward it, and points out that it is prohibited by law everywhere in
the United States. However, the practice is biologically normal, because all mammals show some signs of homosexual behavior. Pomeroy disagrees with the still widely accepted Freudian theory that
homosexuality is the result of fixation at a normal developmental
stage, preferring to see it in terms of Alfred Kinsey's view of human
sexuality as a range or scale, with those who are only heterosexual at
one end and those who are only homosexual at the other, and most
people somewhere in between. He explains that most Americans
tend to perceive the situation in opposites and extremes. "We are
only beginning to understand this extremely complex problem,"
says Pomeroy, "and anyone who says he has 'the' answer must be
taken with a grain of salt." In the meantime, he urges tolerance for
those who are different.

In discussing dating, Pomeroy spends a great deal of time on
every adolescent's fear of rejection, and analyzes the differences in
the expectations and sexual patterns brought to the experience by
the two sexes. Girls think of dating as primarily a social good time,
while boys probably think of it as a means of having some sort of
physical contact with a girl. Petting is something almost everybody

does before marriage. It is pleasurable, a learning experience, a form of communication. To relieve frustration, he recommends masturbation afterward, or petting to orgasm if both parties want it. The real morality of petting is that it should be mutual—a boy should never force a girl to go further than she desires. The same is true of the decision to have intercourse or not. Again he gives a detailed list of pros and cons; in the last analysis, a person who feels comfortable about a decision to have sex should be able to be discreet or to face society's disapproval. *Boys and Sex* remains one of the most sensible and careful sex education books yet written, and if it were not that changes in the abortion laws have outdated the section on that subject, it would still be useful today.

Girls and Sex, on the other hand, is invalidated by a tinge of sexism in Pomeroy's acceptance of the roles society imposes on women. Published in 1969, it is completely different from *Boys and Sex*. Unlike most other authors of companion volumes, who simply lifted whole chapters from the first work and made only minor adjustments to adapt it to the other sex, Pomeroy carefully rewrote nearly every word. In an introduction for parents, he addresses the special anxiety fathers and mothers feel over their daughters' sexuality.

> Parents tell me they are teaching their daughters to be "ladylike." That means the social amenities—to be feminine, demure, nonagressive, to keep their dresses down and their legs crossed, and not to chase the boys. In the society we live in these are generally considered desirable attributes, but they are not attributes which lead toward a good sexual adjustment in marriage unless they are accompanied by teaching her to be a warm, open, responsive, sexually unafraid person. A young woman must unlearn her ladylike conduct in the bedroom and there revert to her more unrestrained nature in order to become a sexually responsive wife."

His message for the girls themselves is similar. In the first chapter he again presents his own credo, which he has clarified since writing *Boys and Sex* the year before. Whether or not to engage in sexual activity must be an individual's own decision, and should be based on as much information as possible, he begins. The purpose of *Girls and Sex* is to provide that information: "My feeling is that sexual behavior for both girls and boys is something both pleasurable and desirable as long as certain rules are followed. The rules are simple: 1. Nothing is done to hurt someone else or to go against their wishes and desires—in brief, responsibility for the other person. 2. Whatever is done is not done so openly that it will get a girl or a boy into trouble with society. On the other side of the coin, I would respect those who choose *not* to engage in any sexual experiences. That is their right."

Pomeroy examines in some detail the common differences in attitude between the sexes. Boys, with their earlier experiences with orgasm, tend to be genital-oriented, while girls react to the romantic ambience of sex. A girl needs to understand these differences, because:

> A girl will come to understand she must be something of an actress in life. It will be clear that she has been given three roles to play. One is her role in society, first as a young girl growing up, then as a wife and mother, or as a career girl, or both, whatever the case may be. The second role is her relationship with boys, in which, as I have said, she must learn to be both ladylike and, eventually, unladylike when that kind of behavior is required. The third role is perhaps the most difficult—the role she must play as herself, an individual responsible to herself.

The chapter on physiology deals with girls' worry about the size of their breasts and has more extensive information on menstruation than that provided for boys. The section on childhood sex play is also adapted for girls' information needs. In addition to the reassurance about the normality of such play, Pomeroy deals with the troublesome but seldom-mentioned topic of sexual advances from older men—often uncles or fathers of friends, as well as strangers.

Dating can be less of a problem for girls if they keep in mind those important differences between the sexes. It is unfortunate that society makes it necessary for a girl to be constantly concerned with her reputation: "As long as it is necessary to play the ridiculous game of 'good girl,' 'bad girl' and 'prude,' I suppose the best thing a girl can do is confront squarely the kind of face she wants to present to the world and develop her dating behavior accordingly." With this caution in mind, petting receives qualified approval as a preparation for intercourse at a later stage. Girls may not enjoy it particularly when they first begin, but will soon find out what stimulates them best. Here Pomeroy offers a more sensible reason for a girl to slow the boy down—not because petting is bad in any way, but because she needs time to catch up to his level of arousal. Pomeroy again stresses mutuality as the measure of petting morality.

Perhaps the most important precedent set by *Girls and Sex* is a factual and informed chapter on "The female orgasm." Tackling a subject that had been nearly unmentionable in teen sex literature, Pomeroy carefully undoes the myth of the vaginal orgasm, and explains the physiology of stimulation and response of the clitoris. He refers often to the findings of Masters and Johnson and to statistics from his own research—telling girls, for instance, that, although parents may not like to hear it, "it is demonstrably true that girls who have orgasm when they are young—that is, up to fifteen—are those who have the least difficulty having one in marriage later on." He shares what was then known about multiple orgasms, and defines a nymphomaniac as "a woman who has a higher rate of sexual outlet than the person who calls her that name." Orgasm is a learned response, and girls should not be disappointed if they do not have one the first time they try. "Orgasm should not be viewed as a tyrant"; the important thing is the feeling of closeness and the shared pleasure of intercourse. The rest of the book presents information on masturbation, homosexuality, birth control, and the decision of whether or not to have intercourse with the same objectivity that was given to boys.

The slight sexist tendencies of *Girls and Sex* are inevitable for a book written in 1969—Pomeroy was far more sympathetic and fair-minded toward girls than most of his fellow sex educators at the time. Both his books are perceptive and intelligently written; it is to be hoped that his publishers will soon encourage him to make the small adjustments necessary for a second edition, so that another decade of teenagers can have the benefit of these best of the modern sex education books.

## BIBLIOGRAPHY

Bauer, William W. *Moving into Manhood.* Garden City, NY. Doubleday, 1963.

———, and Bauer, Florence M. *The Way to Womanhood.* Garden City, NY: Doubleday, 1965.

Bausch, William J. *A Boy's Sex Life; A Handbook of Basic Information and Moral Guidance.* Notre Dame, IN: Fides Publishers, 1969.

Bohannan, Paul. *Love, Sex, and Being Human; A Book about the Human Condition for Young People.* Garden City, NY: Doubleday, 1969.

Bracher, Marjory Louise. *Love, Sex, and Life.* Philadelphia: Fortress Press, 1964, rev. ed., 1966.

Bueltmann, A. J. *Take the High Road.* St. Louis, MO: Concordia Publishing House, 1967.

Burn, Helen Jean. *Better than the Birds, Smarter than the Bees; No-nonsense Answers to Honest Questions about Sex and Growing Up.* Nashville, TN: Abingdon Press, 1969.

Cain, Arthur H. *Young People and Sex.* New York: John Day Co., 1967.

Duvall, Evelyn Ruth Millis. *Love and the Facts of Life*. New York: Association Press, 1963.

Fribourg, Arlette. *Every Girl's Book of Sex*. New York: Arc Books, 1967.

Glassberg, Bertrand Younker. *Barron's Teen-age Sex Counselor*. Woodbury, NY: Barron's Educational Series, 1965.

Gottlieb, Bernhardt S. *What a Boy Should Know about Sex*. Indianapolis: Bobbs-Merrill Co., 1960.

––––––. *What a Girl Should Know about Sex*. Indianapolis: Bobbs-Merrill Co., 1961.

Hamilton, Eleanor. *Sex before Marriage: Guidance for Young Adults, Ages 16–20*. New York: Meredith Press, 1969; New York: Bantam, 1973.

Hettlinger, Richard Frederick. *Living with Sex: The Student's Dilemma*. New York: Seabury, 1966.

Hulme, William Edward. *Youth Considers Sex*. New York: Nelson, 1965.

Johnson, Eric W. *Love and Sex in Plain Language*. Philadelphia: Lippincott, 1965; rev. eds., 1967, 1973, 1977.

Kelly, George, *The Catholic Youth's Guide to Life and Love*. New York: Random House, 1960.

Kelly, George A. *Dating for Young Catholics*. Garden City, NY: Doubleday, 1963.

Landers, Ann (pseud. of Esther P. Lederer). *Ann Landers Talks to Teen-agers about Sex*. Englewood Cliffs, NJ; Prentice-Hall, 1963.

Levinsohn, Florence. *What Teenagers Want to Know*. Chicago: Budlong Press, 1962.

Lewis, Wade V. *Sex: In Defense of Teen-agers*. Boston: Christopher Publishing House, 1967.

Lorand, Rhoda L. *Love, Sex, and the Teenager*. New York: Macmillan, 1965.

McGinnis, Tom. *A Girl's Guide to Dating and Going Steady*. Garden City, NY: Doubleday, 1968.

Masters, William H., and Johnson, Virginia E. *Human Sexual Response*. Boston: Little, Brown, 1966.

Mazur, Ronald Michael. *Commonsense Sex: A Basis for Discussion and Reappraisal*. Boston: Beacon Press, 1968.

Oraison, Marc. *Learning to Love; Frank Advice for Young Catholics*. Trans. by Andre Humbert. New York: Hawthorn Books, 1965.

Peck, Ellen. *How to Get a Teen-age Boy and What to Do with Him when You Get Him*. New York: Bernard Geis Associates, 1969; New York: Avon, 1974.

Pemberton, Lois Loyd. *The Stork Didn't Bring You!*, 3rd ed. New York: Nelson, 1965.

Pomeroy, Wardell Baxter, with Tebbel, John. *Boys and Sex*. New York: Delacorte Press, 1968; New York: Dell, 1971.

––––––. *Girls and Sex*. New York: Delacorte Press, 1969; New York: Dell, 1973.

Public Affairs Committee. *Teen Love, Teen Marriage*. New York: Grosset and Dunlap, 1966.

Puner, Helen Walker. *Not While You're a Freshman.* New York: Coward-McCann, 1965.

Schoenfeld, Eugene. *Dear Doctor Hip Pocrates; Advice Your Family Doctor Never Gave You.* New York: Grove Press, 1968.

Shedd, Charlie W. *The Stork Is Dead.* Waco, TX: Word Books, 1968.

Southard, Helen E. *Sex before Twenty: New Answers for Youth.* New York: Dutton, 1967; rev. ed., 1971.

Taylor, Gerald J. *Adolescent Freedom and Responsibility; A Guide to Sexual Maturity.* New York: Exposition Press, 1965.

Wier, Frank E. *Sex and the Whole Person: A Christian View.* New York: Abingdon Press, 1962; rev. ed., 1965.

Witt, Elmer N. *Life Can Be Sexual.* St. Louis, MO: Concordia Publishing House, 1967.

# 8

# *Instant Obsolescence in the Seventies*

In the early seventies, sex educators began to evaluate the impact that the social and political changes of the previous decade had had on sexual attitudes and behavior in America. For the first time, a body of empirical data existed on the physiology of the sex act. The pill had made it possible to separate coitus from the procreative function, and women were now able to have sexual experiences as casually as men if they wished. Newly interpreted freedoms of speech made it possible to print words never before seen in most publications, to illustrate birth control methods with drawings and photographs, and to show realistic nudes. A new concern for the equality of women had opened up exploration of what it really means to be female—and male. The laws on abortion and the rights of minors were beginning to be changed. Experiments in communal living and group marriage had suggested that the nuclear family might not be the only valid way to set up long-term sexual unions. Although the sexual revolution had jarred loose many old attitudes and beliefs, a residue of fears and taboos still clung, and some sex educators continued to reflect those fears in their works for young people. This reluctance to keep abreast of rapid social changes made much of their work subject to instant obsolescence.

Venereal disease and unwanted pregnancy, both now avoidable, were still often presented as punishments and deterrents to any sexual activity at all, rather than mishaps of a badly managed sex life. Instead of providing more detailed and realistic advice on the cure and prevention of disease and methods of contraception, writers emphasized the worst effects of both conditions. In the face of a mass of statistics showing a high incidence of premarital intercourse, some writers continued to insist that the only socially acceptable sex took place within marriage. Others modified the limitation; they approved sex in relationships characterized by "deep caring," but maintained that casual sex was manipulative and psychologically harmful—at least to girls. Homosexuality was the subject in which the most radical changes in attitude took place during the seventies. Starting from the position taken by Evelyn Duvall (that almost everybody has homosexual feelings and experiences but only homosexuals are homosexual), sex educators gradually turned away from the definition of homosexuality as an illness and began to place it within the context of normal sexual behavior.

Many of the books examined in this chapter either have been invalidated by time or, despite their relative merits, never achieved wide acceptance. Some works that are outdated in their earlier editions but have since been revised have been included in the list of recommended titles in Chapter 9 if their current editions are useful.

Among the sex education books published in 1970, three were curiously old-fashioned in style, if not in content: Understanding Sex by Alan F. Guttmacher; The Facts of Sex; A Revolutionary Approach to Sex Instruction for Teenagers by John James (a pseudonym); and A Teenager's Guide to Life and Love by Dr. Benjamin Spock. Understanding Sex comes close to beginning with the birds and bees approach. Guttmacher, a retired obstetrician and president of the Planned Parenthood Federation, was seventy-two at the time of its writing, and while his attitudes are remarkably liberal for a man of his generation, his style is best described as kindly but garrulous. The book tells far more than any teenager wants to know about obstetrical procedures, for instance, or the details of reproductive anatomy. Guttmacher is opposed to anything more than kissing between casual friends: "To make serious petting justifiable behavior there must be the element of feeling, of emotional involvement, of commitment to each other. In essence, in our culture mature and healthy people care deeply before becoming involved in sex whether heavy petting or sexual intercourse." Guttmacher sees sexuality as part of a behavior continuum, with heterosexuality spanning the greatest part of that range; he estimates that only 4 percent of men and 1 or 2 percent of women are homosexuals, with bisexuals making up "a relatively small group." He freely admits that there is "no clear-cut cause" for homosexuality, but offers "disturbed parent-child relationships" ("the combination of an overattached, seductive mother and an absent, weak, or rejecting father") as a possible explanation. He sees lesbianism as a "safety valve" for girls who are afraid of heterosexual contacts. Such a life is "certainly not to be encouraged" because it carries "dreadful penalties." Guttmacher, as might be expected from the head of Planned Parenthood, is informative about birth control methods (although here, as in the rest of the book, there are no diagrams or photographs). He emphasizes that the use of contraceptives should be a moral obligation for couples who have no desire to produce a child.

The books by James and Spock were not really addressed to young people, in spite of their titles. Nor did James's The Facts of Sex represent a "revolutionary approach" to sex education, being little more than a superficial essay on various aspects of sexuality. Although in A Teenager's Guide to Life and Love, Spock does make occasional attempts to speak to young readers, for the most part he merely offers advice and comfort to parents. In a section on the rivalry between the sexes, Spock's Freudian bias and his theories on the proper care of small children lead him into some resounding sexism. He implies that women compete with men because of penis envy, and suggests that contemporary women are overeducated: "Quite a few women nowadays, especially some of those who have gone to college, find the life of taking care of their babies and children all day boring and frustrating. I think that the main reason so many mothers are bored is that their upbringing and their education have made them somehow expect to get their satisfaction and their pride as adults from the same occupations outside the home as men." Dr. Spock was soon to rue these and similar words, when such remarks were vehemently attacked by leaders of the women's movement.

Also published in 1970, Sex: Telling It Straight by Eric Johnson was "directed to boys and girls who are growing up in places where hardship is one of the facts of life." The book spoke simply to young teenagers growing up in urban ghettos or in isolated rural areas about the basics of sex and love, and dealt with many problems ordinarily considered to be outside the experience of middle-class people (incest, for instance: "If a member of your family tries to have sexual intercourse with you, you should tell someone who can try to get help at once"). Although Johnson stressed the stereotyped male and female role expectations, he was innovative in including a two-way glossary that provided the slang equivalents for standard sex terms, and vice versa. Such a list was an obvious need in sex education, but in 1970 many public librarians were still too shy of four-letter words to add this book to their collections. In the same year, Johnson's Love and Sex and Growing Up was also published, which was an adaptation for preadolescents of his earlier Love and Sex in Plain Language. A revised edition of Sex: Telling It Straight appeared in 1979, and will be discussed in Chapter 9.

## "Facts about Sex": Reflections of the Seventies

*Facts about Sex; A Basic Guide* by Sol Gordon was the most important sex education book published in 1970, not only because it marked the advent of a writer who was to become the voice of the seventies as Duvall had been the voice of the fifties, but because in its four editions the book closely followed the many changes in sexual attitudes of the decade. In its latest edition, entitled *Facts about Sex for Today's Youth* (1973, 1978), it is the most useful simple book in the field.

A clinical psychologist, Gordon is professor of child and family studies and director of the Institute for Family Research and Education, a program of Syracuse University's College for Human Development in upstate New York. For the past ten years he has been a prolific writer and speaker on sex as it relates to children and adolescents. *Facts about Sex* was originally published in 1969 with the title *Facts about Sex for Exceptional Youth*, and was designed to be used with retarded or learning-impaired teenagers. Quickly realizing that there was a need for such a simple book among normal teenagers who were unskilled or unwilling readers, Gordon adapted the book for more general distribution the next year. In an "introduction for parents and youth," he explains that "knowing too much" does not lead to sexual misbehavior. Quite the reverse is true: "Most books about sex are written to please parents who have Victorian views." In this book he will be brief and limit himself to the physical facts of sex, and also will include the "so-called dirty words" where they are relevant. And brief it is—twenty-two pages of text in all, with most chapters only one or two pages of large type.

*Facts about Sex* is saved from condescension by Gordon's straightforward style and by the exquisite nudes and anatomical charts drawn by Vivien Cohen. The first page gets down to basics immediately with a definition of sexual intercourse ("This is when the man inserts his penis into the woman's vagina") and a list of slang synonyms for that function. He outlines conception and birth (with drawings that illustrate the birth process), and male and female sexual anatomy, menstruation, wet dreams, and masturbation ("compulsive" masturbation is a sign of tension). He touches on venereal disease and illegitimate pregnancy, explaining in a footnote that abortion, now legal in some states, is a better choice than bearing an unwanted child. Gordon is not permissive about casual sex for the young and emphasizes the link between love and sex: "Without love, 'making out' or intense physical contact short of sexual intercourse is often not a pleasant experience. It could lead to an increase of tension rather than provide an outlet for sexual urges. It is better to wait until you are an independent adult and in love before having sexual relations."

Under "Sex problems" he mentions child molesters, rape, prostitution, impotence, frigidity, and homosexuality, which he points out is illegal. Slang terms for homosexual are "faggot," "queer," and "gay." For prevention of pregnancy he suggests the pill ("not suitable for everyone"), the diaphragm, or the condom, but cautions that contraceptives are not 100 percent effective. The last chapter consists of the ten most common questions that Gordon has been asked by teenagers. In answer to "Do you think it's right to have sexual intercourse at our ages?" he invokes the "risk of unhappy or tragic consequences," but concedes that "older working or college youth who love each other and can easily arrange for contraceptives and privacy may want to make their own decisions about premarital sex." Other questions concern venereal disease, oral sex, the meaning of "cherry," and "What causes homosexuality and can it be cured?" It is not caused by any one thing, he answers, and is not uncommon, but a few experiences do not make one a homosexual.

Published in 1973, the third edition, entitled *Facts about Sex for Today's Youth*, contains considerable changes. It was in that year that a U.S. Supreme Court decision legalized abortion in America. Ruling on the cases *Roe* v. *Wade* and *Doe* v. *Bolton*, the Court declared that all state laws that prohibit or restrict a woman's right to obtain an abortion in the first three months of pregnancy were unconstitutional. Also, the American Psychiatric Association changed its official definition of homosexuality from "mental disorder" to "sexual orientation disturbance," a term that was now applied only to "those who wish to change their sexual orientation." In a press release on December 15, the association declared that "Homosexuality in and of itself implies no impairment in judgment, stability, reliability, or vocational capabilities."

Both events are reflected in Gordon's revision. A reference to the illegality of abortion has been removed and the section on homosexuality (formerly headed "Sex problems," now headed "Sex problems and differences") has been expanded. Gordon explains that psychologists no longer "see 'voluntary' homosexuality as a problem or disorder," and adds the clarification that "Most boys and girls have homosexual thoughts occasionally." The words "lesbian," "dyke," and "butch" have been added to the slang vocabulary list, and Gordon explains that religious and professional groups are opposed to laws that interfere with private sexual behavior.

Perhaps the most noticeable change in *Facts about Sex for Today's Youth* is in the illustrations—black and oriental teenagers are now included in a genre that had previously ignored these audiences. In the "Author's introduction" the "Victorian" parents have become "uptight" parents. New research, says Gordon, shows that "many (if not most) teenagers will have sex before marriage without parental knowledge or consent"; while he acknowledges this behavior, he assures parents that he does not advocate it. In the first chapter, a drawing of the female external genitalia has been added, thus introducing the clitoris, and the description of masturbation adds the sentence "The clitoris is a source of sexual pleasure for the woman both in masturbation and during intercourse." The age for female puberty has been lowered from 12 to 10 or 11. "Some young people" who have sex before marriage has been adjusted to "many young people."

Whereas the first edition had described premarital sex as "something that is not right," Gordon now refers to "enjoying" sex thoughts, and shares the new finding that women may have gonorrhea without obvious symptoms. To the list of birth control methods he adds foam and intrauterine devices and some very clear pictures of various contraceptive techniques and apparatus. In the question section the query about the meaning of the word "cherry" is gone, and in its place is an inquiry about the boundaries of normal and abnormal sex. To the information about venereal disease he adds that almost all states now permit treatment of minors without parental consent.

Five years later the changes in the 1978 edition of *Facts about Sex for Today's Youth* are fewer but similarly significant. The book is adorned with completely new drawings by Vivian Cohen that retain the multiracial theme and are still lovely. The words on homosexuality now appear under the heading "Sex differences," and stress that such behavior is no longer considered a disease or a disorder. Gordon continues to give the slang terms for homosexuals, but distinguishes between those words that are "popular" and those that are "negative." Bisexuality and lifelong celibacy as valid sex choices are also mentioned in this section. Other minor changes emphasize that abortion is preferable to teenage pregnancy, and that sexual intercourse is not the most important expression of love. Herpes is now discussed in the section on venereal disease, and Gordon has added the rather odd observation that immature love affairs are tiring but the real thing is energizing. The bibliography emphasizes books, tapes, and filmstrips produced by Gordon himself. In this edition the book is currently useful, and appears in the annotated list in Chapter 9.

Several authors of older books issued new versions in 1971. Helen Southard, whose *Sex before Twenty* had been conservative in 1967, produced an equally conservative update. Gladys Shultz, who had proffered advice to a college daughter via the U.S. mail in *Letters to Jane* (1948), now corresponded with a college granddaughter in *Letters to a New Generation*, to the effect that most recent changes in social thinking and behavior, from the use of drugs to the emphasis on clitoral orgasm, were deplorable. *Our Sexual Evolution* by Helen Colton took the opposite tack in an approving once-over-lightly of the new attitudes. *The Sex Book; A Modern Pictorial Encyclopedia* by Martin Goldstein undoubtedly had many teenage readers, although it was not addressed to them. Arranged in dictionary format, it displayed a surfeit of photographs of human genitals and copulating couples in an astonishing variety of positions.

An even more surprising title was *Facts o' Life Funnies* (1972), edited by Lora Fountain and distributed by the Multi Media Resource Center of San Francisco. This was a comic book that presented some cautionary tales about sex with cheerful obscenity. The first story, for instance, is "Fat Freddy Gets the Clap," drawn by Gilbert Shelton, dean of underground comic artists. Although the book was highly effective at communicating basic sexual hygiene to teenagers, most parents and librarians found it coarse and objectionable.

The use of the comic book as sex education was further developed by Sol Gordon in 1975 with the publication of a book with the breathless title *You! The Psychology of Surviving and Enhancing Your Social Life, Love Life, Sex Life, School Life, Home Life, Work Life, Emotional Life, Creative Life, Spiritual Life, Style of Life, Life.* The book was based on a collection of previously published comic books (including *Ten Heavy Facts about Sex, Protect Yourself from Becoming an Unwanted Parent, V.D. Claptrap, Gut News for Modern Eaters, Juice Use,* and *Drug Doubt*), which Gordon had first distributed independently. Roger Conant provided the crude but effective drawings and some horrendous puns, and Gordon provided the serious data. The combination was eye-catching and irresistible to teenagers, and although not as deliberately obscene as *Facts o' Life Funnies,* the comics were offensive enough to alarm conservative authorities. (In 1971, when representatives from the Institute for Family Research and Education of Syracuse University distributed free copies of one of the earlier titles to teenagers at the New York State Fair, they were soon stopped by the management, and not until Gordon had seen the matter through the courts were they allowed to return in 1974.) Employing the nonlinear, free-form style of the comic books it was based on, *You!* caught the spirit of the time. It remains a mainstay of today's sex education collection, and will be further annotated in Chapter 9.

Another collection that was taken very seriously was *Our Bodies, Ourselves* (1976) by the Boston Women's Health Collective. Originally produced by a feminist group with medical advisers, it was an assemblage of detailed information and firsthand testimonials about the workings of the bodies of women. Although it was not really addressed to teenagers, the book was enthusiastically endorsed by many feminist librarians, and the issue of its use with adolescents soon became politicized. The contents undoubtedly were useful in part for young women, and the issue will soon be resolved by the publication of a new but similar book by some of the same editors that is intended solely for teenagers.

## Liberal Guides to Sex Enjoyment for Teenagers

*Youth and Sex: Pleasure and Responsibility* by Gordon Jensen (1973) was an extremely liberal book with a strangely inconsistent chapter on homosexuality that perpetuated old myths and stereotypes. The rest of the book is informed, aware, sympathetic, and even somewhat erotic. Jensen begins with a list of sexual words followed by "other words that mean the same thing" and their definitions. For "intercourse" he gives thirty-one equivalent terms, most of them vulgar, and then says drily, "Notice that there are a lot of words for this act of sexual behavior. They all mean that the penis is put into the vagina." The illustrations are also extraordinarily frank—photographs of a nude young couple holding hands, a close-up photo of the vulva, both closed and spread open to show the internal structure, and a picture of the same young couple examining an unrolled condom. Jensen discusses the benefits of masturbation, and provides a detailed and realistic description of intercourse. He approves of petting if both parties are willing, although he advises that a girl should not become more involved sexually than is comfortable for her.

Jensen endorses the condom as the cheapest, most efficient, and most easily available contraceptive, and tries to overcome some of the common resistance to it, even recommending that girls carry one or two of them for emergencies. He does not attempt to discourage premarital intercourse, saying "Several strong arguments can be made against virginity"—it handicaps initial sexual adjustment in marriage, for one. In general, "each person has to come to terms with his own moral convictions and conflicts in the matter of premarital intercourse." A chapter on legal abortion discusses methods and costs, the position of the Catholic Church, and possible psychological reactions. In view of Jensen's fundamentally permissive stance in *Youth and Sex*, it is surprising to find him insisting that "homosexuals often are quite maladjusted mentally and socially. Almost all of them have short-range goals, and much of their behavior is self-defeating. The life of a homosexual is dismal compared with the life of a normal heterosexual person."

An even more liberal book, perhaps the most liberal teen sex education book yet published, was *The Sex Handbook; Information and Help for Minors* (1974) by Heidi Handman and Peter Brennan. Addressing their book to teenagers under eighteen, the authors provide "practical information that's hard to get—information about your body, about having sex, about getting birth control . . ." but they say nothing about love because "you already know your own feelings better than anybody else." The style is direct and colloquial and the stress is on enjoyment and avoiding interference from authority figures: "Parents, schools, churches, and even the government try to make it as difficult as possible to enjoy your own body." There are separate chapters on losing your virginity ("How to have intercourse for the first time—how to make it easier and more enjoyable"), female orgasm, and advanced techniques like oral and anal sex. The chapters on birth control, abortion, and venereal disease discuss not only methods but how teenagers can get advice and care on their own: "The care and feeding of sex organs" explains what to expect of a gynecological examination and the symptoms and treatment of common infections, while a chapter on sex and the law explains such matters as the rights of emancipated minors and the meaning of statutory rape. The book ends with a useful but quickly outdated "directory of services in every state where people under eighteen can get birth control, pregnancy tests, VD tests, general medical care, abortions, abortion referrals, legal help, and counseling with sexual problems." This hedonistic approach severely limited the book's acceptability to most parents and librarians, however, and it was denounced by several reviewers for dealing with sex "only from the neck down."

An equally pragmatic book that was not so alarming was *Sex and*

*Birth Control; A Guide for the Young* (1973) by E. James Lieberman and Ellen Peck (the same Ellen Peck who in 1969 had written *How to Get a Teenage Boy and What to Do with Him when You Get Him*). The authors point out that the old scare tactics have not been effective in controlling venereal disease and illegitimacy, and propose that "it is time to change from 'don't' to 'it depends' when talking about premarital sex." In assisting this transition, they offer a long (299 pages) and thorough discussion of modern methods of pregnancy prevention and venereal disease control. The book would still be useful except for the recommendation of the now-suspect Dalkon Shield IUD and the changes in abortion laws.

In 1973 Eric Johnson revised *Love and Sex in Plain Language* (1965, 1967). This edition is slightly expanded and the new illustrations by Russ Hoover are not quite as effective as the sepia drawings of the earlier editions. A few other changes in this edition are slight but significant. The chapter on female anatomy now comes *before* that for the male; the function of the clitoris has been added to the description of intercourse; orgasm is described as "a glorious spasm"; the chapter called "Husband and wife unite in sexual intercourse" is now titled "Man and woman unite in sexual intercourse"; information on legal abortion has been added; and the discussion of fertilization explains principles of heredity and the function of chromosomes.

More important is the inclusion of a new chapter on the differences—and similarities—between male and female sexuality that discusses sex role expectations: "People have come more and more to want to be free, free to be themselves, whichever sex they may belong to. They are less willing to play unthinkingly the role of man or woman that our society encourages. In other words, we are coming to see that in each of us there is some of what we think of as the masculine and some of what we think of as the feminine." The greatest change is Johnson's complete revision of the chapter on homosexuality. Now titled "Homosexuality—being 'gay' " rather than "Some special problems of sex," the chapter is a model of compassionate thinking on the subject. Johnson defines a new term here—homophobia: "the strong, unreasoning fear of homosexuality, not unlike racial or religious prejudice." He explains that heterosexuals are called "straight" as distinguished from "gay," that female homosexuals are often called "lesbians," and that there are many people who are bisexual. He speaks approvingly of the gay liberation movement, and says "many homosexual men and women are happy and satisfied and are managing to make successes of their lives." A further revision of *Love and Sex in Plain Language* appeared in 1977 and is included in the annotated list of current titles in Chapter 9.

A pair of books with a conservative stance that quickly dated them were *Sex and Sensibility: A New Look at Being a Woman* (1974) by Elizabeth M. Whelan and *Making Sense out of Sex: A New Look at Being a Man* (1975) also by Elizabeth M. Whelan in collaboration with her father-in-law, Stephen T. Whelan. Both Whelans have M.P.H. degrees from the Yale School of Medicine. In these books they stress their opposition to any sex whatsoever for teenagers. Homosexuality is described as "definitely not normal" and is linked with molestation in the volume for boys. In the volume for girls the word "homosexual" appears only in the glossary, and "lesbian" not at all. Birth control is discussed only in the context of marriage, and venereal disease is seen as a punishment for illicit sexual activity. Loss of virginity is equated with promiscuity. Although girls are told they "may" choose a job or career, marriage is presented as a woman's most important objective. Both books reinforce the traditional masculine and feminine role stereotypes.

*Psyching out Sex* (1975) by Ingrid Rimland, a book about the psychological and emotional aspects of sexuality, was marred by a dreary format and a wordy style. The author, a high school counselor and educational psychologist, wrote thoughtful chapters on the new demands of the women's movement and the homophile movement, and exposed the negative effects that traditional role expectations can have on the personality. Unfortunately, few teenagers had the patience to pursue Rimland's argument through her vocabulary and syntax. In any case, it is not clear that a book of this type is really suitable to the needs of sexual beginners.

In 1977, Dr. Peter Mayle, author of two controversial sex education books for children—*Where Did I Come From?* and *What's Happening to Me?* (both 1975)—wrote a teen sex education book called *Will I Like It?* The publisher kept the large-type picture-book format of the juvenile titles, but replaced the cartoons that had made them so refreshing with some semipornographic photographs. As the title indicates, the book is a how-to guide for teenagers who have decided to have sex and have already picked out a partner. The tone is friendly and not condescending, and some of the advice is highly practical, but the whole is marred by a certain lack of attention to factual detail. Some reviewers also objected to the cover—a large, wrap-around nude. Critics also objected strenuously to Sol Gordon's *You Would if You Loved Me* (1978), a collection of "lines" that boys supposedly use to seduce girls. These ranged from the transparent to the crude, and in some cases Gordon supplied snappy comebacks for girls. Although some librarians found this paperback "witless and repetitive," Gordon's rationale was that forearmed is forewarned.

In *Sex, Love, or Infatuation: How Can I Really Know?* (1978), Ray E. Short, a Methodist minister, deals with the moral issues of sex from a narrowly traditional point of view. He admits to no alternatives to the expected progression of love, marriage, sex and children—in that order. Short believes that the distinction between infatuation and love is crucial, and he presents fourteen chapters of "key clues" for deciding into which category a particular emotion falls. He also provides a list of arguments for and against remaining a virgin until marriage, including "facts" such as "Those who have premarital sex tend to have less happy marriages." The footnotes reveal, however, that the studies cited in support of many of these "facts" date from 1953. While the book might be useful for solacing parents in a very conservative community, it is of negligible value to young adults facing the bewildering variety of sexual choices in the modern world.

Another rigidly traditional book with an even narrower focus is *How to Be Happy though Young* (1979) by Darian B. Cooper. Writing from a Fundamentalist Christian position, the author justifies her conservative advice point by point with quotes from the Scripture. Teens are scrupulously to avoid any sexual activity before marriage ("Keep clear of all sexual sin so that each of you will marry in holiness and honor—not in lustful passion as the heathen do, in their ignorance of God and his ways"—1 Thessalonians 4:3–5), and to eschew dating non-Christians ("Do not be bound together with unbelievers . . ."—2 Corinthians 6:14). Alcohol, cigarettes, and marijuana are lures of Satan, as are astrology and cults like the Children of God or the Moonies. Only those who agree with Cooper's religious beliefs could find her sexual advice at all relevant.

*Straight Talk about Love and Sex for Teenagers* by Jane Burgess-Kohn (1979), which employs the familiar question-and-answer format, is an oddly inconsistent book. The author's attitudes seem to have changed during its writing. The first chapters read like a dating ritual from the fifties, but the next few chapters examine the morality of "premarital sex" for couples who are engaged or at least in love. Burgess-Kohn's underlying assumption is that boys are predators and girls are preyed upon: A girl who "allows" sexual liberties and then discovers that the boy doesn't love her is disgraced. Yet further on the author debunks virginity as a desirable condition for brides, and discusses cohabitation with only mild disapproval. There is a quite detailed description of fellatio, and a relatively informative chapter on homosexuality. The author deplores the idea that the vagina, rather than the clitoris, is the source of female sexual pleasure, yet she describes intercourse as if an internal climax were the expected conclusion for women. The focus is on "thoughts, feelings, and questions that many of you have about love and sex" and very little information is provided about basic physiology. Overall, the mixture of old-fashioned and contemporary attitudes in this book is disturbing and confusing.

## BIBLIOGRAPHY

Boston Women's Health Collective. *Our Bodies, Ourselves*, rev. ed. New York: Simon & Schuster, 1976.

Burgess-Kohn, Jane. *Straight Talk about Love and Sex for Teenagers*. Boston: Beacon Press, 1979.

Colton, Helen. *Our Sexual Evolution*. New York: Franklin Watts, 1971.

Cooper, Darian B. *How to Be Happy though Young*. Old Tappan, NJ: Fleming H. Revell Co., 1979.

Fountain, Lora. *Facts o' Life Funnies*. San Francisco: Multi Media Resources Center, 1972.

Goldstein, Martin. *The Sex Book: A Modern Pictorial Encyclopedia*. New York: Herder and Herder, 1971.

Gordon, Sol. *Facts about Sex: A Basic Guide*. New York: Day, 1970.

———. *Facts about Sex for Exceptional Youth*. Plainview, NY: Charles Brown, 1969.

———. *Facts about Sex for Today's Youth*. New York: John Day Co., 1973; new ed. Charlottesville, VA: Ed-U-Press, 1978.

———. *You Would if You Loved Me*. New York: Bantam, 1978.

———, with Conant, Roger. *You! The Psychology of Surviving and Enhancing Your Social Life, Love Life, Home Life, Work Life, Emotional Life, Creative Life, Spiritual Life, Style of Life, Life*. New York: Quadrangle, 1975.

Guttmacher, Alan Frank. *Understanding Sex: A Young Person's Guide*. New York: Harper & Row, 1970; New York: New American Library, 1970.

Handman, Heidi, and Brennan, Peter. *The Sex Handbook: Information and Help for Minors*. New York: Putnam, 1974.

James, John (pseud.). *The Facts of Sex: A Revolutionary Approach to Sex Instruction for Teenagers*. Princeton, NJ: Vertex, 1970.

Jensen, Gordon D. *Youth and Sex: Pleasure and Responsibility*. Chicago: Nelson-Hall, 1973.

Johnson, Eric W. *Love and Sex in Plain Language*, rev. ed. Philadelphia: Lippincott, 1973, 1977; New York: Bantam, 1974.

————. *Sex: Telling It Straight.* Philadelphia: Lippincott, 1970; rev. ed., 1979.

————, and Johnson, Corinne B. *Love and Sex and Growing Up.* Philadelphia: Lippincott, 1970; New York: Bantam, 1974.

Lieberman, E. James, and Peck, Ellen. *Sex and Birth Control; A Guide for the Young.* New York: Crowell, 1973; New York, Schocken, 1975.

Mayle, Peter. *"Will I Like It?" Your First Sexual Experience; What to Expect, What to Avoid, and How Both of You Can Get the Most out of It.* Los Angeles: Corwin Books, 1977.

Rimland, Ingrid. *Psyching out Sex.* Phildelphia: Westminster, 1975.

Short, Ray E. *Sex, Love, or Infatuation: How Can I Really Know?* Minneapolis: Augsburg, 1978.

Shultz, Gladys (Denny). *Letters to a New Generation; For Today's Inquiring Teenage Girl.* Philadelphia: Lippincott, 1971.

Southard, Helen E. *Sex before Twenty; New Answers for Young People,* rev. ed. New York: Dutton, 1971.

Spock, Benjamin. *A Teenager's Guide to Life and Love.* New York: Simon & Schuster, 1970.

Whelan, Elizabeth M. *Sex and Sensibility: A New Look at Being a Woman.* New York: McGraw-Hill, 1974.

Whelan, Stephen T., and Whelan, Elizabeth M. *Making Sense out of Sex: A New Look at Being a Man.* New York: McGraw-Hill, 1975.

# 9
# *Harvesting the Current Crop*

Sex education books for young adults have come a long way in eighty-seven years—from the first antimasturbation tract in 1892 to books in the late seventies that make an earnest effort to tell teen-agers what every young person should know rather than what every young person should not know. But prejudices and untested assumptions endure. Although this year we may have the illusion that contemporary sex books say what is right and good to say about the subject, as attitudes change and scientific knowledge increases, these books also will seem inadequate.

What standards and criteria can we use to evaluate the older sex education books on library shelves and the new titles in bookstores and publishers' catalogs? Perhaps the most important qualities we can bring to these decisions are an awareness of our own sexuality and information needs and a willingness to keep in touch with changing knowledge and social patterns. A book need not express the most liberal sentiments to be acceptable, nor should it be rejected because it is conservative or radical, but the attitudes it expresses should come within hailing distance of prevailing social opinion and recognize the complexities of a pluralistic society. Factual information is another matter—a book should certainly be eliminated if it contains errors or inaccuracies or if the facts are out of date. Changes in the law or in the knowledge of biological functions or the safety of birth control methods can invalidate a formerly acceptable title. In general, any book over ten years old should be discarded, and even books over five years old should be examined very carefully.

Several lists of recommended titles that represent the careful and informed thought of young adult librarians and sex educators are currently available; these can be especially helpful in evaluating older books. *Sex Is a Touchy Subject*, a pamphlet prepared in 1976 by the Bay Area Young Adult Librarians of California, analyzes nearly one hundred book titles, both fiction and nonfiction, from a liberal feminist orientation. It also discusses recommended films and selected pamphlets. In 1979, Carol Starr and Elizabeth Talbot of the Alameda County Public Library in California adapted and slightly updated the nonfiction section of this bibliography in their article "Sex—Ask the Librarian" in *Collection Development, Library Journal*'s Special Report No. 6.

Outlining their evaluation criteria in this article, Starr and Talbot emphasize the importance of accurate information, but they also believe that format and style should be considered in selecting books. They recommend titles that use nonclinical, everyday words in a writing style that is appropriate to, and establishes a rapport with, the intended reader. Illustrations should help explain the text, and an author's attitude toward homosexuality and the roles of men and women should be considered as an indicator of his or her awareness of recent social change.

Another source, which applies strict evaluative criteria to an exhaustive list of books and pamphlets for teenagers, is the *Guide to Sexuality Handbooks*, produced in 1979 by a joint committee of the Planned Parenthood Federation of America, the American Association of Pediatrics, and the Young Adult Services Division of the American Library Association. The Sex Information and Education Council of the United States (SIECUS) has included an excellent selected list of sex education books for preteens and young adults in the pamphlet *Human Sexuality: Books for Everyone*.

Evaluating new books as they come off the press calls for help from skilled reviewers. A dependable and prestigious source is the bimonthly *SIECUS Report*, which includes reviews of books and films on sex, announcements of workshops and training programs for sex educators, and some thoughtful and informative articles. *School Library Journal* and the American Library Association's *Booklist* also often publish intelligent reviews of new sex education books. The *Voice of Youth Advocates* (VOYA), a magazine written by and for young adult librarians, covers a wide range of subjects, and reviews most teen sex education titles.

# Evaluation Sources for Sex Education Books

## Booklists

*Guide to Sexuality Handbooks.* Planned Parenthood Federation of America, American Association of Pediatrics, and Young Adult

Services Division of the American Library Association, 1979. Order from YASD, ALA, 50 E. Huron St., Chicago, IL 60611.

*Human Sexuality: Books for Everyone.* Reprinted from the *SIECUS Report*, January 1976. 2–49 copies, 10¢ each; 50 or more copies, 5¢ each. Order from SIECUS, 137-155 N. Franklin St., Hempstead, NY 11550.

*"Sex—Ask the Librarian." Collection Development.* LJ Special Report No. 6. 1979. $5 per copy, or $3.95 cash with order. Send to *Library Journal*, R. R. Bowker Co., 1180 Ave. of the Americas, New York, NY 10036.

*Sex Is a Touchy Subject: A Select Bibliography of Books, Pamphlets, and Films on Sex and Sexuality for Young Adults.* Bay Area Young Adult Librarians, 1976. $2 per copy, $2.50 if billed. Order from BAYA, c/o Richard Russo, 2343 San Juan Ave., Walnut Creek, CA 94596.

*Review Magazines*

*Booklist.* Semimonthly. $20 per year. Order from the American Library Association, 50 E. Huron St., Chicago, IL 60611.

*School Library Journal.* Monthly September through May. $17 per year. Order from R. R. Bowker Co., Subscription Dept., Box 67, Whitinsville, MA 01588.

*SIECUS Report.* Bimonthly. $10 per year. Order from Human Sciences Press, 72 Fifth Ave., New York, NY 10011.

*Voice of Youth Advocates.* Monthly. $11 per year. Order from VOYA, 10 Landing Lane, Apt. 6M, New Brunswick, NJ 08901.

Why is it so important to make sure that the very best sex education books are available for teenagers? Because the ability to relate sexually to other human beings is a major, perhaps *the* major, learning experience of the adolescent years. And up to now we have failed dismally in providing young people with the information and guidance that will help make them happy and responsible sexual beings. Gonorrhea has reached epidemic proportions, and syphilis lags not far behind. *Eleven Million Teenagers*, a pamphlet published in 1976 by the Alan Guttmacher Institute of the Planned Parenthood Federation, contains page after page of statistics that prove that we have failed to motivate and inform teenagers even about the relatively simple subject of contraception:

U.S. teenage childbearing rates are among the world's highest, topped
only by Romania, New Zealand, East Germany, and Bulgaria.

Of the 21 million young people in the United States between the ages of
15 and 19, more than half are estimated to have had sexual intercourse.

Each year more than one million 15- to 19-year-old women become pregnant, *one-tenth of all women in this age group.*

Two-thirds of these teenage pregnancies are unintended.

Half of sexually active, never-married teenagers said that they did not
use a contraceptive the last time they had intercourse.

Leading reasons for not using contraceptives were ignorance of risk of
pregnancy or unavailability of birth control.

Even where sex education is taught in schools, birth control is covered in
only 39 percent of the classes.

The search for more effective sex education methods and information tools must persist. The following annotated bibliography is a
guide to sex education books that this author considers to be the best
titles currently available to teenage readers.

# Sex Education Books for Right Now

Comfort, Alex, and Jane. *The Facts of Love; Living, Loving and
Growing Up.* New York: Crown, 1979. 128 pp. $10.

In *The Facts of Love,* the authors of *The Joy of Sex* communicate
their sense of celebration about the pleasures of sexuality, but with
an emphasis on responsible, caring behavior. The book is unique in
being the first teenage manual to sanction recreational sex. According to the Comforts, "sex in humans has three uses—reproduction,
relation and recreation (in other words, babies, love and fun). And
this is the origin of a lot of the crossed wires and worry which have
made one of the best things in life into one of the most anxious for
humans. YOU NEED TO KNOW WHICH OF THESE THREE YOU ARE AFTER,
AND WHICH YOUR PARTNER IS AFTER." Sex just for play is fine, they
maintain, if both people know they are playing, if each is concerned
that the other has a good experience, and if birth control is used.
Throughout the book the responsible use of birth control is a major
theme. The Comforts recommend a combination of sheath and foam
because these methods are most easily available to teenagers and
because the combination distributes responsibility equally between
the partners. However, in the preface for parents they suggest the pill
as the preferable contraception method for young people who have

access to adult assistance. The authors firmly convey the importance of this concern for people by stating: "There are two really wicked and immoral sexual acts, which you should be ashamed to commit if you are a human being. One is deliberately to produce, or risk producing, a baby you don't want and can't rear. The other is to treat another person as a thing simply because you like their body and want to play with them, without making sure they want that too."

The Comforts also take a firm stand against alcohol as "the most dangerous drug of addiction in modern society" and urge that young people promise themselves never to drive a car or have sex if they have been drinking at all. Some of the Comforts' statements here may prove controversial. They assert that pornography is harmless and enjoyable (although "It often contains a lot of exaggerated or anxious ideas about sex"), and refer to bisexuality as the natural human state ("though our society doesn't encourage it"). They also approve of public nudity in appropriate circumstances.

Like *The Joy of Sex*, this book is illustrated with handsome drawings of people caring for each other, but without the specifically erotic content of the adult volume. The format of the book—large pages with wide margins and clear type—is very pleasing, although the modified picture-book shape may give the impression that the book is addressed to a younger audience than it is. The Comforts have aimed the text at eleven-year-olds and up on the premise that the information they provide should be introduced at puberty. However, they suggest that older teenagers may also find the book helpful.

Demarest, Robert J., and Sciarra, John J. *Conception, Birth and Contraception, A Visual Presentation*, 2nd ed. New York: McGraw-Hill, 1976. 145 pp. $12.

This is a slim but excellent pictorial presentation of human sexual anatomy. Especially effective in the second edition (it was first published in 1969), the book uses beautiful drawings, most of them full-page, and a very brief text to explain the physiology of sex. It includes pictures of a birth sequence and depicts the various methods of contraception and abortion. Useful as a supplement to books that focus primarily on ethics.

Eagan, Andrea Boroff. *Why Am I So Miserable if These Are the Best Years of My Life? A Survival Guide for the Young Woman*. Philadelphia: Lippincott, 1976. 251 pp. $7.95; rev. ed., New York: Avon, 1979. 220 pp. $2.25.

In *Sex Is a Touchy Subject*, the Bay Area Young Adult Librarians call this book "A clear, modern look at being a teenage woman, which acknowledges current male chauvinistic attitudes while presenting the idea of other equally valid choices." Writing from a strong feminist position Eagan encourages young women to be self-determining, stresses the value of friendships with other young women, and exposes the aim of the advertising establishment to make women feel anxious about the way they look. Along with the usual information about physiology, menstruation, venereal disease, and birth control, she includes a detailed explanation of what to expect from an internal gynecological exam, and an analysis of which IUDs are unsafe. Eagan's statement on sex and love is in striking contrast to earlier books:

> Sex doesn't necessarily go with love. You can have sex (of any variety) just because you feel like it, whether you love the person (or even like him) or not. Two people can be physically attracted, have great sex together, and have very little else in common. Once again, what you do in a situation should depend on what you want to do, what will make you happy, and not on someone else's ideas of what you should or shouldn't do. You are always the best judge of your own feelings.

Gordon, Sol. *Facts about Sex for Today's Youth*, rev. ed. Charlottesville, VA: Ed-U-Press, 1978. 44 pp. $2.50.
 A short and deceptively simple book that presents all of the essential information in an attractive and dignified format. Its clear, concise text makes it useful with unskilled or unwilling readers, while its forthrightness, lack of condescension, and handsome illustrations give it appeal for all sexual beginners. There are also a number of minor changes in wording and emphasis in this edition, and one major change: The section on homosexuality has been substantially rewritten to clarify that homosexuality is not a disorder or a disease, but an acceptable life choice.

Gordon, Sol, with Conant, Roger. *You! The Psychology of Surviving
 and Enhancing Your Social Life, Love Life, Sex Life, School Life,
 Home Life, Work Life, Emotional Life, Creative Life, Spiritual
 Life, Style of Life, Life*. New York: Times Books, 1975. 142 pp.
 $6.95.
 A rambling anything-goes collection—relating loosely to the theme of being a (sexual) human being—of poems, lists, cartoons, engravings, drawings, photographs, observations, personal credos, anecdotes, jokes, aphorisms, and blank pages to write on. Bound in are six comic books that use crude drawings and raunchy humor to convey basic cautions about sex, diet, alcohol, and drugs. The book's modish approach is lent credibility by Gordon's status as a leading

sex educator. Although somewhat flip and irreverent, *You!* is undeniably attractive to teenagers and fun to browse through.

Hamilton, Eleanor. *Sex, with Love; A Guide for Young People.* Boston: Beacon Press, 1978. 174 pp. $10.95, pap. $3.95.

This radical but responsible book has a deceptively conservative format with no anatomy diagrams or photographs. The emphasis is on understanding sex as an activity between two people who want to give each other pleasure. Repeating the philosophy first expressed in her 1969 book, *Sex before Marriage,* Hamilton approves of masturbation as a way to learn the body's responses, and she suggests petting to orgasm as the most practical approach to lovemaking for sexual beginners. Hamilton describes intercourse in terms of both male and female patterns, with emphasis on the more complex female response. The chapter on same-sex relationships starts with the assumption that everybody is capable of loving both sexes; the way that people choose to express that love is a result of society's pressures and their own life experiences. Unorthodox sex is divided into those behaviors that exploit other people—rape, exhibitionism, voyeurism, child molesting—and those that are nobody's business but the participants—transsexuality, transvestism, fetishes, and brother-sister incest. Recognizing that sexuality encompasses not just genital contact but a person's whole life, Hamilton urges young people to touch each other with affection and to learn the art of massage. Most radical of all, she recommends that young adults initiate a frank talk with their parents, and ask for the right to have comfortable and safe sex with their partners in their own rooms behind locked doors.

Hettlinger, Richard F. *Growing Up with Sex.* New York: Seabury, 1971. 162 pp. $4.95, pap. $3.95.

In spite of its age, this remains an intelligent and thoughtful presentation of the conservative position. Speaking from within the framework of liberal Episcopalian attitudes, Hettlinger feels that sexual union should be sanctioned by at least the intent to marry, although he says that the "immorality" of premarital sex has been exaggerated. Instead, he stresses mutual consideration and concern in relationships. In a chapter on homosexuality he carefully differentiates between adolescent homosexual acts and feelings and lifelong homosexuality; while he maintains that the gay life may be difficult and biologically unfulfilling, he supports the right of homosexuals to live without unfair social and legal discrimination. The book is notable for clearly recommending petting to orgasm as the preferred sexual behavior for teenagers. Matters other than ethics are dealt with in appendixes on sex organs, birth control, and venereal disease. The discussion of abortion here is worded in such a way that it has not been invalidated by the 1973 legalization.

Hanckel, Frances, and Cunningham, John. *A Way of Love, a Way of Life; A Young Person's Introduction to What It Means to Be Gay.* New York: Lothrop, Lee & Shepard, 1979. 156 pp. $7.95.

A book that has long been needed, this sex manual for homosexual young adults presents an insider's view of gayness. The authors deal with such problems as how to tell parents and friends that you are gay and how to meet other gay people. A history of homosexuality stresses the homophile nature of ancient Greek civilization, and the legal and medical problems special to gays are dealt with at some length. Sources of information, counseling, and gay pride organizations are also discussed and young gays are urged to seek help if they need it. The chapter on sexual activity is especially striking in its complete freedom from role identification: "Sexual activity is basically the same for everyone" say Hanckel and Cunningham, and go on to prove it by describing the range of human possibilities in the sex act, regardless as to whether the partners are of the same or the opposite sex. The tone is empathetic and practical, and the authors incorporate a good deal of anecdotal material derived from their own experiences and from the experiences of their gay friends.

Hunt, Morton M. *The Young Person's Guide to Love.* New York: Farrar, 1975. 181 pp. $6.95. New York: Dell, 1977. $1.50.

Hunt's book is not really a sex education handbook, but an exploration of the range of human emotions as related to sexual experience. Interesting and simply written. *Sex Is a Touchy Subject* says, "All kinds of love—gay and straight, sadism and masochism, May-December romances, etc. The author urges readers to be tolerant of other people's relationships, no matter how strange they may seem."

Johnson, Eric W. *Love and Sex in Plain Language,* 3rd rev. ed. Philadelphia: Lippincott, 1977. 143 pp. $6.95.

Written in a spare and simple style for junior high teenagers, this book has been outstanding through all its four editions. The first edition (1965) is examined in detail in Chapter 7, and subsequent revisions are discussed in Chapter 8. This latest version retains Johnson's clear writing, concern for persons, and good sense of organization while correcting his earlier sexism. The chapter on homosexuality is exemplary. While providing the necessary information on physiology, Johnson also is quite clear about the basic ethic of moral sexual behavior: "Never forget that human beings are not made to be used." The only significant change from the 1973 edition is a rewording of the paragraph on rape, to make it more sympathetic to the victim.

Johnson, Eric W. *Sex: Telling It Straight,* rev. ed. Philadelphia: Lippincott, 1979. 112 pp. $7.95.

This new edition of Johnson's 1970 title is no longer specifically addressed to young people in urban ghettos or in isolated rural areas, although the contents have not changed much. Johnson has also dropped the prominent glossary of street slang that got him into trouble with teachers and librarians. The book still speaks with simple directness to young teenagers about basic sexual matters. The stress on stereotyped sex role behavior has been softened by the addition of a section that explains that "men and women are becoming more equal" and that it is now acceptable for a couple "to act the way they feel like acting, . . . not just the way everybody used to say a man or a woman should act." In a chapter titled "Some other problems of sex," Johnson discusses not only molesters, rape, incest, and prostitution but also the problem of sex used selfishly. While not quite so fashionable as other recent titles, this book remains a classic for its simple dignity and warmth.

Kelly, Gary F. *Learning about Sex; The Contemporary Guide for Young Adults,* rev. ed. Woodbury, NY: Barron's Educational Series, 1977. 188 pp. $8.95, pap. $3.50.

*Learning about Love* is the best general purpose sex education book available today for older teenagers. Kelly, a sex counselor, clearly and objectively explains many of the complex psychosocial aspects of sexual behavior. Without offering advice, he presents the moral issues within the perspective of our pluralistic society, and provides self-quizzes and discussion questions to help young people think through their own positions. This is undoubtedly the most egalitarian book of the current crop. Changing concepts of masculinity and femininity are explored; the information on the clitoral function is helpful and accurate; and Kelly discredits the theory that girls are slower to become aroused and therefore should be responsible for limiting the couple's sexual activity. There is a thorough and sympathetic discussion of homosexuality in the chapter titled "Different strokes for different folks." Changing attitudes toward marriage are examined and alternative ways of structuring a committed relationship are described with attention to their potential benefits and pitfalls. Kelly gives well-selected lists of further reading at the end of each chapter, and provides a glossary of "four-letter and other words." Although the emphasis is on the interpersonal aspects of sex, biology is not neglected. Clear and complete information on anatomy, birth control, venereal disease, the sexual response cycle, and other essential topics is an important part of this excellent guide.

McCoy, Kathy, and Wibbelsman, Charles. *The Teenage Body Book.*
    New York: Pocket Books (Simon & Schuster), 1978. $5.95.

The authors of *The Teenage Body Book*—a former editor of *Teen* magazine and an adolescent medical specialist—use a letters-to-the-editor format to put sexuality in a perspective of total mind and body health. Beginning with "Dear Doctor: Am I Normal?" the topics range through woman's body, man's body, the changing feelings of adolescence, weight control, exercise, sports injuries, plastic surgery, health habits, psychosomatic illness, and special medical needs of teenagers such as advice on anorexia nervosa, scoliosis, and Osgood-Schlatter disease. Sexuality is seen as integral to the whole personality, and not just a matter of genital function: "Accepting your sensations, your fantasies, your desires, your feelings—from tenderness to passion—as normal and natural can help you to feel more at ease with others and with yourself. Your sexuality is you— the man, the woman, the person." Masturbation is praised as a healthy release; it only becomes a potential problem if a person feels guilty about it. However, "If you choose not to do so, due to your personal beliefs, that doesn't make you strange." Even group masturbation or the use of props is given qualified approval.

A broad spectrum of research and attitudes on homosexuality is presented, with quotes from the findings of prominent sex researchers and a testimony from a young lesbian. In the final analysis, "the real question is not whether you're gay or straight, but how you manage your relationships." In the discussion on intercourse, the authors reassure nonparticipators: "As a free—and certainly acceptable—choice virginity is definitely OK," even if "there are times when you begin to feel like the last virgin on earth over the age of 14." After a competent and thorough discussion of birth control methods, venereal disease prevention and cure, abortion (including possible psychological reactions), and pregnancy, the book closes with an extensive list of resources: Planned Parenthood clinics, departments of adolescent medicine, gay services, and help centers for special problems such as alcoholism, asthma, epilepsy, drug abuse, and rape. Unfortunately, the lack of an index limits the book's usefulness.

Mintz, Thomas. *Threshold: A Doctor Gives Straightforward Answers to Teenagers' Most Asked Questions about Sex.* New York: Walker, 1978. 120 pp. $7.95.

A fairly conservative simple and basic guide for junior high teenagers, written by a psychiatrist at the University of California Medical School. Each topic—anatomy, pregnancy, birth control, venereal disease—is given a brief introduction, which is then followed by twenty or thirty questions and answers, presumably extracted from Mintz's experiences in teaching a sex education class for adolescents. The questions reflect the fears of very young teenagers: "What if I'm afraid to masturbate?" "Does it hurt to menstruate?" "How old will I be when I start to ejaculate?" and "What do you do if you grow up and discover you just don't like having sex?" There are only two questions on homosexuality, and the answers imply that some homosexuals can get cured through psychoanalysis. Nothing is included on street vocabulary, rape, or deviations.

Winship, Elizabeth C. *Ask Beth; You Can't Ask Your Mother.* Boston: Houghton Mifflin, 1972. 244 pp. $6.95, pap. $4.95.

A warm and sensible collection of answers to letters from teenagers by the author of the newspaper column "Ask Beth." Winship comes down slightly on the conservative side of such issues as homosexuality and premarital sex, but with humor and compassion. The abortion information predates the Supreme Court decision that made it legal, but this is only slightly troublesome in context. In addition to the usual topics of pubertal changes, petting, going steady, venereal disease, and birth control, Winship offers useful advice on matters of grooming, parents, school, drugs and alcohol, and interracial dating.

# INDEX